Con~~grat~~ ~~ulat~~ions

Patty

U N U S U A L
& MOST POPULAR

Baby
Names

Cleveland Kent Evans, Ph.D.
American Name Society

This Is Your
First Baby Name
Book From: Jesi

Author: Cleveland Kent Evans, Ph.D., annually conducts one of the most comprehensive surveys on name usage in the United States. His current work in given names involves personality, social psychology, anthropology, and popular culture. He has written many articles for scholarly and popular publications and has been interviewed on radio and television. Dr. Evans is currently associate professor of psychology at Bellevue College in Nebraska. He is a member of the American Name Society.

Table of Contents

What Will We Name Our Baby?

Long before your baby is born, you begin to think about a name that will be exactly right. Your child will be wearing this name for a lifetime, so you have a unique and important responsibility. This book is designed to help you name your baby. It lists hundreds of names for boys and girls and provides brief explanations of the origins of the names and their variations. We've also identified some of the famous and successful people who have borne the name, along with a few well-known fictional characters. In addition, the 1,000 most popular names are ranked according to their frequency, based on an extensive recent survey.

In this introduction you'll learn about the history and psychology of names and how people from some other countries name their babies. You'll also find a complete explanation of the way in which we determined a name's popularity. This information will help you study the lists of names and find the ones you like. Choosing a name for your baby is an important decision; this book will help you find the name that best fits your child.

What's In a Name?

Should you be concerned about whether your child has a common or an unusual first name? Is it better to have one or the other? Psychologists and sociologists who have examined these questions for years still disagree on the answers.

On the one hand, a great deal of evidence shows that strong and direct impressions are created about what sort of person will use a particular name, based solely on the name itself, prior to meeting the actual person. Most Americans, for example, expect *Chad* to be handsome and athletic; *Jacqueline* to be sophisticated and successful; and *Bertha* to be fat, loud, and overbearing. Research has found that teachers may give a higher grade to a school paper by a student named *David* than to one by *Elmer*—even though the papers are identical. And photos of pretty young women called *Jennifer* or *Kathy* are more likely to win a beauty contest when compared with pictures labeled *Gertrude* or *Harriet*. Studies show that children as young as seven, as well as college students and adults, begin shaping an opinion about someone based on the perceived desirability of his or her name. Many of these same studies have found a strong correlation between the frequency of use of a name in our culture and its rated desirability, especially when boys' names are concerned.

On the other hand, studies that compare *actual people* with common first names to other people with unusual names often show that those with unusual names enjoy an advantage. People with uncommon first names are more likely to be listed in *Who's Who,* for example, and are more successful as psychologists. College women with unusual first names score higher on scales of sociability and self-acceptance. They are also more likely to have a positive sense of individuality, which helps them resist peer pressure.

Why do these different studies seem so contradictory? Part of the answer is that the first set of studies forced people to form impressions based entirely on the name alone. In contrast, recent research shows that including information about an actual person compensates for most of the negative effects of a stereotype and creates a different context in which to view the name. For example, if told that we were going to meet a man called *Igor*, most of us would conjure up the image of an ugly, stupid, and evil character like Frankenstein's henchman. But if Igor turned out to be a handsome and intelligent young man who explained that his parents had admired the composer Igor Stravinsky, we would very likely find his name to be intriguing and sophisticated.

Another reason for the contradictory results from such studies is that uncommon names and names with negative images are not necessarily the same. Boys called *Derry* or *Tate* and girls called *Calista* or *September* will have a chance to create their own first impressions, free from preconceived ideas. They can develop a positive, individual self-concept that is unhampered by the negative images that go along with names like *Adolph, Griselda, Minnie,* or *Percival*.

In the final analysis, of course, your choice of a common or an unusual name depends on your own ideas about what is best for your child. After all, there are many occasions in life, such as submitting an application for a job or seeking admission to college, when a name *does* have a chance to create a positive image on its own. Having a popular name like *Jessica* or *Matthew* at such times might be an advantage. If, on the other hand, individuality and creativity are especially important to you, then an unusual name might be a better choice. Even an unusual name with a somewhat outdated image like *Floyd* or *Gladys* can work if you carefully explain to your child the positive reasons why it was chosen. To learn that he or she was named after an appealing fictional character or an accomplished relative might boost a child's self esteem in unimaginable ways.

Whichever line of thought you follow, remember that a name is much more than just a neutral label. The names you give your children will become lasting and very important parts of their self-image. Obviously, the selection of a "desirable" name for your child does not guarantee happiness and success. But names with a clearly negative or ridiculous image like *Charmin, Devious, Frenzy, Melancholy, Mischief, Nausea, Shackles,* or *Thumper* (all of which were actually conferred upon children born since 1980) will certainly make life much more difficult for those who bear them.

How We Name Our Babies

Everyone has a name, but the customs of naming are different and reflect the habits of the culture in which we live. In China, for instance, names are frequently selected from a poem that contains the names of all the traditional families of "the hundred houses." Other Chinese names often refer to social conditions at the time of birth. For example, many children born during the communist Cultural Revolution of the late 1960s received names like *Yan-Hong,* meaning "aim to be Red."

In Iceland, the father's first name is passed on to the child as a last name with the addition of *-son* (son of) or *-dottir* (daughter of). This means that last names change with every generation: Einar Jonsson's children will be Stefan Einarsson and Kristin Einarsdottir. As a result of this custom, the telephone directory in Iceland is alphabetized by first names, not last names. In France, until recently a baby's name had to be selected from a list approved by the Justice Ministry in order to be legally recorded, and local registrars can still refuse to record a name they don't like.

In the United States and Canada, where many diverse cultures mix together, a variety of naming practices flourish that are influenced by family, ethnic, historical, and religious considerations as well as by personal customs and beliefs. Native Americans have a wide variety of naming practices: Many use names based on events or characteristic behavior (recall the name given to Kevin Costner's character and the title of his award-winning movie, *Dances With Wolves*). Certain names may have symbolic meanings known only to members of a tribe. In some cases names are changed at important transitional times, such as during puberty or at the time of marriage.

Recent immigrants to the United States and Canada often follow the naming customs of their native countries for a time. After one or two generations, however, they usually adopt English-style names. The choice of a given name is sometimes influenced by religious custom. Roman Catholics, for example, often name their children after saints. Most Jews traditionally use names of deceased relatives but never living ones. On the whole, however, parents in the United States and Canada choose names for their children based on purely personal reasons.

Names Today

Currently, parents feel free to bestow just about any name they wish on their unsuspecting offspring. Fortunately, most parents are extremely conscientious about the names they give their children. In fact, ignoring tradition and other restrictions has encouraged parents to look to new sources for names, and this has contributed to the popularity of many imaginative names.

Many people continue to choose traditional names, then alter them with unconventional spellings. As a result, you'll find many variations of names in this book. *Denise*, for example, can be spelled at least four other ways: *Denice, Deniece, Denisse,* and *Denyse.* Note that a change in spelling does not mean that a new name has been created, however, nor will the pronunciation necessarily change.

While strict gender identifications once were the rule, today, many names are used for both girls and boys. Examples of such names include *Adrian, Ashton, Kelly, Leslie, Randy, Robin, Shawn, Taylor, Terry,* and *Tony.* Other names like *Ashley, Aubrey, Kelsey, Lindsey,* and *Whitney,* which were common for boys a generation ago, are now given almost exclusively to girls. Gender lines also blur because of the increased use of surnames for girls' first names. Giving a daughter the mother's maiden name as her given name has been a long-standing tradition in the southern United States. But this practice has spread, and now girls in many parts of the country are commonly named *Ashton, Blair, Blake, Carson, Carter, Greer, Madison, Mallory, Taylor,* and *Tierney.*

Where Do Name Fashions Come From?

American parents have been searching for distinctive names for their children for well over

a century, and as a consequence the names chosen have steadily become more varied. An example of this trend can be seen in the frequency
of use of the most popular names. In 1830,
nearly one out of every six American girls was
called *Mary,* but by 1900 only about one out of
every 15 was given that name. Today, in contrast, only about one of every 33 girls receives
the most popular girls' name, *Brittany.*

Parents looking for new names usually say
they want something "different, but not *too* different." This means, for one thing, that newly
popular names often originate from a slight shift
in the sound of previously popular names. That's
how *Kelsey* has suddenly become so common
for girls: It blends the sounds of *Kelly* and
Chelsea, which were already in vogue.

A second way name fashions are generated
is through the mass media, especially by adopt-
ing the names of well-known fictional characters. This has been going on for quite some time.
Edna and *Earl* were popular names in the late
nineteenth century because Edna Earl was the
heroine of *St. Elmo,* a popular novel by Augusta
Evans Wilson. (She was to authors of that time
what Danielle Steele is to contemporary writ-
ers.) In the early twentieth century, movies
began to have a great influence on names, and
the reach of Hollywood led to the popularity of
first names of stars such as Gary Cooper, Judy
Garland, Carole Lombard, Colleen Moore, and
Gloria Swanson.

Since the 1950s, television has become *the*
dominant influence on American first names,
and the rankings of many of the names on the
Top 500 list were inspired by television shows.
Appealing characters on many types of programs have started or reinforced name fash-

ions. Westerns like *Bonanza, Gunsmoke*, and *Here Come the Brides* popularized *Adam, Benjamin, Jason, Jeremy, Joshua,* and *Matthew*; while dramas like *Dallas* and *Dynasty* made *Alexis, Blake, Crystal (Krystle), Jenna,* and *Kristen* popular. *WKRP in Cincinnati* and *Family Ties* turned *Bailey* and *Mallory* into girls' names in the United States. The television miniseries *North and South* led to the appearance of many *Ashtons* and *Orrys*. In 1990, six times the number of *Ethans* were born in the United States as in 1988, undoubtedly because of characters on *thirtysomething* and *The Guns of Paradise.*

Daytime soap operas have also had a strong influence on the names Americans give their children. *As the World Turns* was the source for many of the *Lisas* born during the 1960s and 1970s, and today the program reinforces the fashions for *Caleb, Lily,* and *Sierra*. Other names promoted by soaps include *Erica, Jeremy,* and *Natalie (All My Children); Ashley, Brock,* and *Nikki (The Young and the Restless); Macy (The Bold and the Beautiful); Hunter* and *Megan (One Life to Live); Eden, Laken,* and *Mason (Santa Barbara);* and *Trey (Capitol).*

When a name introduced on television sounds like other fashionable names, it can go—almost overnight—from obscurity to stunning popularity. The best recent example of this is *Kayla*, which was rare before Kayla Brady appeared as a character on *Days of Our Lives* in 1982. The similarity to *Caitlin, Katie, Kelly, Kyle* and the like immediately caught the attention of parents looking for the "different but not *too* different" alternative. *Kayla* is number 11 on the national list and still rising quickly: It will almost surely be among the top ten American names during the 1990s.

Of course other media besides television have an effect on names. The influence of movies has no doubt increased as a result of the widespread use of VCRs and rented video tapes. *Madison* is one example of a girl's name that achieved popularity largely because of a character in a movie, in this instance the mermaid in the film *Splash*. And in the music world, popular songs by the Beatles and Fleetwood Mac inspired many parents to call their daughters *Michelle* and *Rhiannon*.

Sports heroes naturally play a role in the choices parents make for boys' names: Baseball pitcher Nolan Ryan has many namesakes, and thousands of young African-American males over the last few years have been named after basketball stars Kareem Abdul-Jabbar, Hakeem Olajuwon, Isiah Thomas, Jamaal Wilkes, and Dominique Wilkins.

Names Among African Americans

Since the 1960s, some American blacks have turned to Africa for baby names. *Akinyele* (Yoruba "valor benefits this house"), *Jabari* (Swahili "brave"), *Kwame* (Akan "born on Saturday"), and *Mandisa* (Xhosa "sweet") are examples. Very few genuine African names have become widely popular, however.

Many African-American parents name their children after popular characters on television programs such as *Dominique* on *Dynasty* and *Jaleesa* on *A Different World*. They also honor real-life celebrities like actresses Jasmine Guy and Phylicia Rashad; newscaster Bryant Gumbel; poet Gwendolyn Brooks; singers Sade and the Jackson siblings, Jermaine and LaToya; and comedians Arsenio Hall and Eddie Murphy.

African-Americans also commonly create new names for their children by combining their own sets of fashionable sounds and syllables. Girls' names formed in this way are called *Lakeisha* names after one of the prime examples. Lakeisha names are created by linking a fashionable prefix, like *La-, Sha-, Ka-, Ty-*, and so forth, with a fashionable suffix, such as *-isha, -ika, -onda*, and *-ice*. The resulting names are always accented on the second syllable. Several of these innovative creations, like *Kanisha, Lashonda, Quanisha, Shameka*, and *Shanice*, have become popular enough to make our Top 500 lists. African-American names for boys that are blended this way include *DeJuan, Deontae, Jamar*, and *Tyreek.*

Of course a number of the most popular American names, such as *Ashley, Brian, Brittany, Christina, Christopher*, and *Michael*, have always been used equally by blacks and whites.

Hispanic Names

Americans of Hispanic or Latino origin form one of the largest and fastest-growing groups in our population. Thousands of recent immigrants from Central America, the Dominican Republic, and Colombia are joining the millions of citizens of Mexican, Cuban, and Puerto Rican ancestry already living in this country. It's no wonder that many popular names are brought to us by this growing cultural community.

Hispanic parents traditionally use names for their sons like *Angel, Enrique, Ernesto, Francisco, Jaime, Javier, Jesus, Jorge, Jose, Juan, Julio, Luis, Miguel*, and *Sergio*. Among girls, names such as *Adriana, Araceli, Beatriz, Carolina, Daniela, Gabriela, Isabel, Maria, Na-*

talia, and *Raquel* are common. But there are
many names from other cultures that are more
popular with Latinos than with other Americans.
Stephanie was actually the most popular name
for Hispanic girls in 1990, and other French
names like *Lissette*, *Rene*, and *Yvette* made our
most popular list primarily because of Hispanic
parents. Russian names like *Ivan* and *Tatiana*,
Italian names like *Bianca* and *Giovanni*, and
even traditional English names like *Daisy*, *Edgar*,
Edwin, and *Evelyn* are Hispanic favorites. Still
other names used less often at the moment by
Anglos than by Latinos are *Aileen*, *Claudia*,
Cynthia, *Karina*, *Priscilla*, and *Vanessa* for girls;
and *Ariel*, *Christian*, *George*, *Hector*, *Oscar*, and
Victor for boys. *Antonio* and *Jasmine* are note-
worthy in that they are well liked by both
Hispanics and African Americans while being
much less frequently used by whites.

Regional Differences in First Names

Most of the reported regional variations in
the popularity of first names in the United States
result from differing ethnic compositions. For
example, *Vanessa* is more popular in California
than most other places simply because Hispanics
represent such a large portion of that state's
population. Conversely, African-American names
like *Jamar* and *Tyesha* are very rare in North
Dakota and Vermont, where the black population is very small.

Other regional differences exist, but they do
not always fit the stereotypes that one might
expect. Though Southerners, both white and
black, are a bit more likely than parents in other
regions to give their children unconventional
names, generally the names that are popular

in the South today are the same ones popular everywhere. White Southerners are somewhat more likely than their northern counterparts to have pet names like *Billy*, *Bobby*, *Danny*, and *Eddie* on their sons' birth certificates, but Northerners are more inclined to use forms such as *Carrie*, *Katie*, *Kristi*, and *Mandy* for their daughters.

Much more important than differences between North and South in names are differences between East and West. Parents all along the East Coast are more conservative in their naming patterns than parents west of the Mississippi, and traditional or baby-boomer names like *Christine*, *Jacqueline*, *Linda*, *Mark*, *Mary*, *Patricia*, *Richard*, *Robert*, *Steven*, and *William* are more common in the East. The West, on the other hand, generally picks up newly fashionable names like *Austin*, *Brittany*, *Cody*, *Jacob*, *Kayla*, *Kelsey*, *Lacey*, *Logan*, *Tyler*, and *Whitney* more quickly than the East. Indeed, most new fashions not created by television seem to begin in the West and then move eastward. *Abigail*, *Caitlin*, and *Lauren* are among the occasional exceptions that travel in the opposite direction.

Only a few other regional name patterns have become evident in the 1980s and early 1990s. Traditional Irish-American names like *Bridget*, *Colleen*, and *Kevin* are more common in the northeastern United States, as might be expected from the settlement pattern of Irish immigrants. *Ansley* is now a favorite girls' name with Georgia parents. Utah, with a large Mormon community, has many children named *Camille*, *Dallin*, and *Spencer* after recent Mormon leaders. Residents there also show a special fondness for *McKell*, *Shaylee*, *Shaylyn*, and *Tyson*.

Bradley is especially popular in Missouri, perhaps because Omar Bradley, a famous World War II general, was a Missourian. And for unknown reasons the name *Michaela*, which is just beginning to catch on nationally, has been extremely popular in the state of Nebraska for over a decade.

Most Popular Baby Names: Our Survey

The popularity of a name changes with time and responds to historic events. Thus you can't expect to choose a name for your baby today that will remain as popular or as unconventional in the future as it is now. But names that were common for babies born in 1990 are likely to be well used for at least another decade. The survey of popular names used in this book was conducted by Professor Cleveland Kent Evans of Bellevue College in Nebraska. Conducted during 1990, the latest year for which full data were available from state health departments, the survey included over 794,000 birth records. Accordingly, it provides a good representation from all the main racial and ethnic groups in the population as a whole. Indeed, no other book on baby names makes use of a sample as large and as current. Probably 85 percent of the boys and over 80 percent of the girls born in the United States in 1990 were given names that appear on the Top 500 lists in this book.

Our survey also differs from many others in that the various spellings of a given name were combined together before the rankings were created. For example, our figures for *Brittany*, the number one name for girls, include all girls named *Britany, Britney, Brittanie, Brittney*, and so on. By counting all spellings of a name together, a more realistic estimate of a name's popularity can be achieved than by other studies that count every variation in spelling as a separate name. This is especially true for names like *Kristen/Kristin, Lindsay/Lindsey,* and *Stephen/Steven,* where two spellings are used almost equally. And for names like *Kaeley/ Kaily/ Kaleigh/Kaley/Kaylee/Kayleigh/ Kayley/Kaylie,* where there is absolutely no agreement among American parents as to the correct spelling, a refusal to combine them would invite chaos.

Our alphabetical lists of popular names and their origins include all the important alternative spellings for each name. This should help to make clear just how our popularity rankings were created.

Of course there are vast differences in popularity on our lists between the first name and the 500th. In 1990 about 3.2 percent of American boys were given the most popular name, *Michael* (one out of every 31), but less than one out of every 7,000 was called *Rene,* the last on our list. For girls, *Brittany* accounted for about 3.0 percent of all names for newborns (one out of every 33), while about one out of every 5,400 was named *Lashonda.*

In general, if you give your child a name that is no more common than number 200 on the lists in this book, you will be using a name that appears no more than once in every 2,000 births for that sex. By doing so, names can be avoided that might be considered faddish or conventional for this generation. On the other hand, if you choose a name not on our Top 500 lists at all, you will give your child a name that may be considered creative or unconventional by his or her peers.

Spelling and Meaning

As a glance at the following pages will show, modern parents often look at alternative spellings of a common name as one way to give their child a sense of individuality. But one should probably think twice before using a very unusual spelling of a common name. In the first place, an unconventional variation in spelling by itself really can't provide your child with much distinction: If you name your child *Mycle* or *Bryttknee*, for instance, five other kids will still come running when the teacher calls out the name on the school playground. And though a minor variation such as *Jenifer* for *Jennifer* probably won't cause any difficulty, many people will see an extremely unusual variation like *Genyphur* as a sign, not so much of creativity, but rather of pretentiousness or even illiteracy. If finding a truly individual name is your objective, an authentic variation of the name, like *Jennica* or *Guinevere*, would be a better choice than a one created artificially from a bizarre spelling. If you really want to try an alternative spelling, at least be sure that in the process you don't make your child's name difficult to pronounce.

Another factor parents often consider in deciding on a name is the original meaning of that name. We have tried to provide this information as accurately as possible, but remember that even experts don't agree on the meanings of many of our long-standing names. You should therefore view any interpretation with a grain of salt. You should also remember that the original meaning of a name is not necessarily the same as its meaning today. *Simon*, for example, may have meant "he heard" in ancient

Hebrew, but if it means anything to most Americans today it is likely to be the stereotype of a smart kid who is uncoordinated and wears eyeglasses.

A Word To the Wise

While you are free to give your baby any name you choose, of course, making that decision shouldn't be put off to the last minute. Parents are known to behave irrationally when a baby arrives, and they should remember that a spur-of-the-moment inspiration for their baby's name will affect him or her for a lifetime. Before choosing a name, therefore, take some time to consider a few questions:

• Is the name easy to spell and pronounce?

• What nicknames or pet names can be derived from it?

• Will the initials of the full name form a word? If so, is that word likely to prove embarrassing in any way?

• Does the name truly fit the child's gender?

Keep in mind that a name that's cute for a baby may not age well. We recommend that you give your child a full name rather than a diminutive form of the name: *Katherine Suzanne* is usually preferable to *Katie Sue*. Remember, you can always give a child a nickname and retain the traditional form as the legal name.

Use caution in naming your child after a well-known living person, such as a politician or entertainer. No one can predict the future, and your child might one day be stuck with a name that has acquired a very negative connotation.

Consider your last name carefully, especially if it is hyphenated. Does the first name you've selected flow easily with the middle and last name?

And avoid using first names that are too cute in conjunction with your last name, such as Krystle Ball, Jay Walker, Kitty Katz, Robin Banks, or Harry Mann.

Both parents should agree on the baby's name as much in advance of the due date as possible. Once a decision has been made, stick with it and avoid any last-minute change. Read this book with your partner, make lists of your favorite names, and discuss your reactions. Then write down the names you have selected and take them to the hospital with you. That way you can be sure that the person who fills out the birth certificate does it correctly. Your child will appreciate your thoughtfulness.

Understanding the Baby Name Profiles

The list of boys' names is presented in two parts: the wide range of 500 names from the survey and additional, unusual names that were not part of the survey. Each list is alphabetical. The girls' names are presented in the same way. The following sample entry will help you to understand how to read the lists.

Common spelling
of the name

Origin of the name

Popularity of name
according to survey

Jennifer (14) Cornish form of Welsh *Gwenhwyfar*, from *gwen* [white] + *hwyfar* [yielding, smooth]. Jennifer Capriati (tennis player), Jennifer Jason Leigh (actress). **Gennifer, Jen, Jenifer, Jenna, Jennie, Jenny.**

Famous person, fictional
character, or work of art
with this name

Variations of the name

Top 500 First Names For Boys

Frequency Rank Order:

U.S.A., 1990

Name	Rank	Name	Rank
Michael	1	Alexander	33
Christopher	2	Benjamin	34
Joshua	3	Aaron	35
Matthew	4	Adam	36
James	5	Jeffrey	37
Justin	6	Derek	38
Andrew	7	Richard	39
David	8	Charles	40
John	9	Jeremy	41
Nicholas	10	Travis	42
Steven	11	Nathan	43
Daniel	12	Patrick	44
Ryan	13	Mark	45
Robert	14	Jason	46
Joseph	15	Jesse	47
Jonathan	16	Jared	48
William	17	Samuel	49
Zachary	18	Dustin	50
Brandon	19	Austin	51
Tyler	20	Kenneth	52
Kyle	21	Gregory	53
Anthony	22	Scott	54
Brian	23	Ethan	55
Jacob	24	Bradley	56
Eric	25	Paul	57
Sean	26	Cameron	58
Cody	27	Phillip	59
Jordan	28	Taylor	60
Kevin	29	Shane	61
Thomas	30	Devin	62
Timothy	31	Dylan	63
Corey	32	Alex	64

Name	Rank	Name	Rank
Christian	65	Craig	102
Caleb	66	Carl	103
Ian	67	Luke	104
Marcus	68	Adrian	105
Evan	69	Carlos	106
Trevor	70	Terrance	107
Brett	71	Brent	108
Nathaniel	72	Gabriel	109
Edward	73	Juan	110
Casey	74	Darren	111
Alan	75	Frank	112
Chad	76	Darius	113
Garrett	77	Luis	114
Jose	78	Victor	115
Donald	79	Troy	116
Mitchell	80	Dominic	117
Blake	81	Julian	118
Keith	82	Brendan	119
Ronald	83	Bryce	120
George	84	Larry	121
Vincent	85	Randy	122
Peter	86	Johnny	123
Spencer	87	Isaac	124
Douglas	88	Jeremiah	125
Seth	89	Dennis	126
Wesley	90	Clayton	127
Antonio	91	Russell	128
Logan	92	Jerry	129
Colin	93	Drew	130
Raymond	94	Todd	131
Lucas	95	Terry	132
Chase	96	Levi	133
Curtis	97	Andre	134
Gary	98	Ricky	135
Darryl	99	Randall	136
Joel	100	Tony	137
Colton	101	Louis	138

Name	Rank	Name	Rank
Calvin	139	Walter	176
Skyler	140	Antoine	177
Connor	141	Quintin	178
Jake	142	Maurice	179
Stefan	143	Jamie	180
Dakota	144	Emmanuel	181
Jimmy	145	Marquis	182
Willie	146	Ross	183
Clinton	147	Maxwell	184
Henry	148	Miles	185
Colby	149	Elliott	186
Dalton	150	Jorge	187
Gerald	151	Neil	188
Rodney	152	Terrell	189
Martin	153	Micah	190
Grant	154	Demetrius	191
Jay	155	Danny	192
Jack	156	Albert	193
Frederick	157	Ricardo	194
Lawrence	158	Dwayne	195
Damian	159	Glenn	196
Bobby	160	Arthur	197
Isaiah	161	Bryant	198
Preston	162	Trenton	199
Dominique	163	Reginald	200
Lance	164	Malcolm	201
Tanner	165	Bruce	202
Xavier	166	Theodore	203
Mason	167	Alejandro	204
Mario	168	Rafael	205
Donte	169	Noah	206
Max	170	Hunter	207
Jamal	171	Eddie	208
Billy	172	DeAndre	209
Lee	173	Ronnie	210
Roger	174	Brock	211
Miguel	175	Wayne	212

Name	Rank	Name	Rank
Jesus	213	Dale	250
Elijah	214	Byron	251
Darrion	215	Eugene	252
Cole	216	Jerome	253
Tyrone	217	Jermaine	254
Trent	218	Manuel	255
Jarrett	219	Barry	256
Stuart	220	Leonard	257
Riley	221	Javier	258
Morgan	222	Desmond	259
Alec	223	Ivan	260
Tyson	224	Oscar	261
Edwin	225	Stanley	262
Kurt	226	Brady	263
Giovanni	227	Quentin	264
Marshall	228	Cedric	265
Angel	229	Jackson	266
Tommy	230	Melvin	267
Roy	231	Roberto	268
Zachariah	232	Roderick	269
Chance	233	Deontae	270
Francisco	234	Dean	271
Francis	235	Andres	272
Rashad	236	Damon	273
Courtney	237	Gavin	274
Kendall	238	Brennan	275
Dane	239	Landon	276
Beau	240	Tristan	277
Parker	241	Keenan	278
Harrison	242	Franklin	279
Ruben	243	Clifford	280
Jaron	244	Trey	281
Donovan	245	Harold	282
Braden	246	Wade	283
Marvin	247	Weston	284
Ernest	248	Sebastian	285
Omar	249	Lamar	286

Name	Rank	Name	Rank
Joe	287	Jamar	324
Jerrell	288	Carlton	325
Hector	289	Clint	326
Jarvis	290	Ashton	327
Kelvin	291	Darnell	328
Akeem	292	Tyrel	329
Blaine	293	Leon	330
Gage	294	Julius	331
Ty	295	DeAngelo	332
Kirk	296	Pedro	333
Kendrick	297	Alberto	334
Coty	298	Graham	335
Dallas	299	Alvin	336
Warren	300	Julio	337
Josiah	301	Jace	338
Nelson	302	Lorenzo	339
Corbin	303	Tevin	340
Angelo	304	DeMarcus	341
Eli	305	Ramon	342
Forrest	306	Bernard	343
Hayden	307	Keegan	344
Eduardo	308	Tory	345
Sergio	309	Steve	346
Howard	310	Brenton	347
Kelly	311	Marco	348
Clarence	312	Mohammad	349
Deon	313	Wyatt	350
Shannon	314	Chandler	351
Jaime	315	Malik	352
Earl	316	Orlando	353
Brad	317	Ray	354
Nolan	318	Reid	355
Dexter	319	Marlon	356
Zane	320	Carson	357
Harry	321	Shea	358
Andy	322	Tucker	359
Chaz	323	Sheldon	360

Name	Rank	Name	Rank
Cornelius	361	Quinn	398
Clay	362	Owen	399
Alonzo	363	Chadwick	400
Leroy	364	Heath	401
Fernando	365	Bryson	402
Kalin	366	Sam	403
Alfred	367	Hakeem	404
Jameson	368	Jamil	405
Donnie	369	Tavaris	406
Mackenzie	370	Sterling	407
Tracy	371	Terron	408
DeShawn	372	Freddy	409
Abraham	373	Alexis	410
Edgar	374	Javon	411
Joey	375	Israel	412
Simon	376	Cesar	413
Raul	377	Ralph	414
Alfonso	378	Vernon	415
Armando	379	Marcos	416
Kerry	380	Kareem	417
Roman	381	Thaddeus	418
Lane	382	Cortez	419
Lonnie	383	Fabian	420
Avery	384	DeJuan	421
Marquise	385	Rory	422
Gordon	386	Tremaine	423
Denzel	387	Clifton	424
Dwight	388	Kenny	425
Chris	389	Ezekiel	426
Keaton	390	Shelby	427
Norman	391	Ben	428
Tyree	392	Carter	429
Oliver	393	Herbert	430
Jamel	394	Keon	431
Charlie	395	Khiry	432
Perry	396	Kadeem	433
Enrique	397	Kyler	434

Name	Rank	Name	Rank
Khalil	435	Leslie	468
Diego	436	Gerard	469
Cary	437	Raheem	470
Dallin	438	Will	471
Everett	439	Quincy	472
Felix	440	Sammy	473
Scotty	441	Kiefer	474
Leo	442	Octavius	475
Fred	443	Tobias	476
Marcel	444	Rick	477
Toby	445	Brody	478
Cade	446	Alfredo	479
Dorian	447	DeRon	480
Lloyd	448	Lester	481
Emilio	449	Hassan	482
Amir	450	Wendell	483
Stacy	451	Esteban	484
Kent	452	Ervin	485
Sidney	453	Addison	486
Kellen	454	Don	487
Josue	455	Rasheed	488
Reese	456	Tarik	489
Brant	457	Rakeem	490
Rico	458	Ariel	491
Jackie	459	Leonardo	492
Jean	460	Pierre	493
Kwame	461	Grayson	494
Gilbert	462	Gerardo	495
Noel	463	Ahmad	496
Nico	464	Rudy	497
Lamont	465	Pablo	498
Amos	466	Blair	499
Dontavius	467	Rene	500

Top 500 First Names For Girls

Frequency Rank Order:
U.S.A., 1990

Name	Rank	Name	Rank
Brittany	1	Kelly	33
Ashley	2	Alicia	34
Jessica	3	Crystal	35
Amanda	4	Alyssa	36
Sarah	5	Hannah	37
Megan	6	Allison	38
Samantha	7	Kimberly	39
Stephanie	8	Amy	40
Caitlin	9	Jamie	41
Katherine	10	Laura	42
Kayla	11	Mary	43
Lauren	12	Erin	44
Emily	13	Brianna	45
Jennifer	14	Cassandra	46
Courtney	15	Victoria	47
Rachel	16	Alexandra	48
Nicole	17	Casey	49
Elizabeth	18	Katie	50
Chelsea	19	Anna	51
Amber	20	Taylor	52
Rebecca	21	Whitney	53
Christina	22	Brandi	54
Tiffany	23	Andrea	55
Kristen	24	Jordan	56
Heather	25	Morgan	57
Danielle	26	Haley	58
Lindsey	27	Christine	59
Michelle	28	Angela	60
Melissa	29	Alexis	61
Jasmine	30	Natalie	62
Erica	31	Jacqueline	63
Kelsey	32	Shannon	64

Name	Rank	Name	Rank
Brooke	65	Gabrielle	102
Kaylee	66	Kylie	103
Kristy	67	Margaret	104
Candace	68	Kirsten	105
Tara	69	Patricia	106
Lisa	70	Kendra	107
Kara	71	Dana	108
Leah	72	Leslie	109
Sierra	73	Tabitha	110
Molly	74	Gina	111
Holly	75	Sydney	112
Maria	76	Anne	113
Vanessa	77	Hillary	114
Paige	78	Bianca	115
April	79	Michaela	116
Stacy	80	Theresa	117
Alexandria	81	Carrie	118
Olivia	82	Devon	119
Lacey	83	Katrina	120
Shelby	84	Bridget	121
Miranda	85	Caroline	122
Abigail	86	Jaclyn	123
Natasha	87	Karen	124
Jenna	88	Mallory	125
Carly	89	Jillian	126
Breanna	90	Sabrina	127
Julia	91	Madeline	128
Julie	92	Mackenzie	129
Monica	93	Diana	130
Marissa	94	Cynthia	131
Bethany	95	Savannah	132
Melanie	96	Abby	133
Ariel	97	Kaylyn	134
Felicia	98	Robin	135
Krista	99	Veronica	136
Kathleen	100	Carissa	137
Desiree	101	Emma	138

Name	Rank	Name	Rank
Shaina	139	Sasha	176
Kiara	140	Tanisha	177
Shawna	141	Janelle	178
Chantel	142	Susan	179
Cassie	143	Amelia	180
Destiny	144	Deborah	181
Grace	145	Cori	182
Tracy	146	Raven	183
Valerie	147	Joanna	184
Alexa	148	Arielle	185
Deanna	149	Heidi	186
Autumn	150	Elise	187
Mercedes	151	Jenny	188
Carolyn	152	Alanna	189
Jocelyn	153	Karla	190
Renee	154	Lydia	191
Kanisha	155	Barbara	192
Claire	156	Gabriela	193
Audrey	157	Meredith	194
Jessie	158	Nikki	195
Madison	159	Adrienne	196
Monique	160	Tiara	197
Melinda	161	Yesenia	198
Keri	162	Leticia	199
Ebony	163	Linda	200
Angelica	164	Trisha	201
Dominique	165	Jade	202
Angel	166	Chanel	203
Adriana	167	Iesha	204
Bailey	168	Kierra	205
Tamara	169	Sandra	206
Katlyn	170	Ciara	207
Aubrey	171	Ellen	208
Tasha	172	Misty	209
Callie	173	Denise	210
Colleen	174	Christian	211
Keisha	175	Jaleesa	212

Name	Rank	Name	Rank
Camille	213	LaTasha	250
Sherry	214	Marisa	251
Virginia	215	Ali	252
Chloe	216	Tori	253
Nancy	217	Jerrica	254
Marie	218	Breanne	255
Mariah	219	Regina	256
Kiana	220	Taryn	257
Ariana	221	Leanna	258
Hope	222	Alisa	259
LaToya	223	Angelina	260
Leanne	224	Carmen	261
Toni	225	Tanya	262
Porsha	226	Kari	263
Justine	227	Kira	264
Lakeisha	228	Wendy	265
Rachelle	229	Cassidy	266
Summer	230	Brianne	267
Shayla	231	Shante	268
Brenda	232	Kirstie	269
Cheyenne	233	Sharon	270
Tierra	234	Faith	271
Tia	235	Asia	272
Tina	236	Tamika	273
Maggie	237	Tonya	274
Karina	238	Melody	275
Nina	239	Tessa	276
Sophia	240	Corinne	277
Tiana	241	Kiersten	278
Janae	242	Kate	279
Pamela	243	Jodi	280
Raquel	244	Randi	281
Shaniqua	245	Dawn	282
Simone	246	Mia	283
Priscilla	247	Rose	284
Sonya	248	Maegan	285
Ashton	249	Mandy	286

Name	Rank	Name	Rank
Anastasia	287	Shanika	324
Shelly	288	Kali	325
Martha	289	Shanna	326
Alaina	290	Beth	327
Tatiana	291	Alice	328
Suzanne	292	Lillian	329
Skylar	293	Rochelle	330
Shanae	294	Bobbi	331
Chasity	295	Julianne	332
Charlene	296	Loren	333
Naomi	297	Paula	334
Terri	298	Cecilia	335
Shanice	299	Sylvia	336
Charlotte	300	Mindy	337
Cheryl	301	Gloria	338
Angelia	302	Cindy	339
Leigh	303	Frances	340
Donna	304	Lena	341
Maya	305	Cherise	342
Lori	306	Sheena	343
Carol	307	Shea	344
Selena	308	Sade	345
Linsey	309	Sheila	346
Jill	310	Evelyn	347
Janet	311	Daniela	348
Joy	312	Jane	349
Annie	313	Susanna	350
Macy	314	Carolina	351
Antoinette	315	Denisha	352
Sadie	316	Dorothy	353
Bonnie	317	Kady	354
Jana	318	Tammy	355
Kendall	319	Helen	356
Ruth	320	Codi	357
Cherie	321	Claudia	358
Diane	322	Danica	359
Clarissa	323	Jeanette	360

Name	Rank	Name	Rank
Ashlyn	361	Lily	398
Nikita	362	Eva	399
Serena	363	Alexia	400
Marah	364	Marcy	401
Alia	365	Jackie	402
India	366	Latifah	403
Kami	367	Janessa	404
Precious	368	Nicolette	405
Sally	369	Celeste	406
Miriam	370	Elaine	407
Rosa	371	Elisa	408
Larissa	372	Yolanda	409
Eileen	373	Jamila	410
Blair	374	Riley	411
Juliana	375	Kathy	412
Dena	376	Isabel	413
Alysia	377	Noelle	414
Elisha	378	Maura	415
Keely	379	Joanne	416
Charity	380	Genevieve	417
Ruby	381	Josie	418
Alyse	382	Lissette	419
Chantal	383	Tamesha	420
Marina	384	Shaylee	421
Whitley	385	Patrice	422
Yasmin	386	Rhonda	423
Lucy	387	Alina	424
Johanna	388	Rikki	425
Shameka	389	Maureen	426
Brenna	390	Micah	427
Roxanne	391	Shirley	428
Esther	392	Reyna	429
Elena	393	Maryann	430
Cecily	394	Kyra	431
Cherelle	395	Shakira	432
Natalia	396	Misha	433
Kyla	397	Laurel	434

Name	Rank	Name	Rank
Lara	435	Beatriz	468
Marilyn	436	Melisa	469
Daisy	437	Sherika	470
Alex	438	Hallie	471
Quanisha	439	Justina	472
Janice	440	Kia	473
Audriana	441	Elissa	474
Annelise	442	Eliza	475
Nadia	443	Sandy	476
Diamond	444	Kenya	477
Cameron	445	Talisha	478
Rhiannon	446	Ansley	479
Adrian	447	Francesca	480
Stevie	448	Gretchen	481
Dakota	449	Tyler	482
Beverly	450	Paris	483
Candy	451	Gianna	484
Shaylyn	452	Jacy	485
Charlee	453	Lashay	486
Darci	454	Michal	487
Ayana	455	Charmaine	488
Tawny	456	Ryan	489
Skye	457	Rosemary	490
Betty	458	Nakia	491
Deidra	459	Bryn	492
Yvette	460	Marsha	493
Constance	461	Nakisha	494
Adrianne	462	Marisela	495
Lynn	463	Kamisha	496
Anita	464	Janie	497
Yvonne	465	Zoe	498
Shawnee	466	Laken	499
Amberly	467	Lashonda	500

Most Popular
<u>Boys' Names</u>

Aaron (35) Hebrew *Aharon*, uncertain meaning, perhaps "mountain" or "shining." Aaron Burr (third U.S. vice president), Aaron Copland (composer). **Aron, Arron, Ehren, Erin, Ron, Ronnie.**

Abraham (373) Hebrew *Avraham*, "father of many." Abraham Lincoln (16th U.S. president). **Ab, Abbran, Abe, Abie, Abram, Avraham, Bram, Habran, Ham, Ibrahim.**

Adam (36) Hebrew *adama*, "earth, clay." Adam Clayton Powell (member of Congress), Adam Smith (economist). **Ad, Adan, Adano, Adao, Addy, Adkin, Atkin, Edom.**

Addison (486) Middle English *Addisone*, "son of **Addy** (a form of **Adam**)." Addison Mizner (architect). **Adison.**

Adrian (105) Latin *Hadrianus*, "from the Adriatic." Adrian Belew (musician), Adrian Bolt (conductor). **Adrain, Adrean, Adriano, Adrianus, Adrien, Adriento, Adrin, Hadrian.**

Ahmad (496) Arabic "more praiseworthy." Ahmad Rashad (sportscaster). **Ahmaad, Ahmod.**

Akeem (292) Probably a Nigerian form of **Hakeem. Ahkeem, Akheem, Akhiem, Akiem.**

Alan (75) Celtic, uncertain meaning, perhaps "rock"; introduced into England in 1066 by the Normans. Alan Jay Lerner (lyricist and playwright), Alan Shepard (astronaut). **Alain, Alano, Allan, Allen, Alun, Alyn.**

Albert (193) Old German *Adalbert*, "noble and bright," from *athal* [noble] + *berhta* [bright]. Albert Gore (45th U.S. vice president), Al Jarreau (singer). **Adel, Al, Alberdo, Albertino, Alberto, Albertus, Albrecht, Bert, Del, Delbert, Hab.**

Alberto (334) Spanish and Italian form of **Albert**. Alberto Salazar (marathon runner), Alberto Tomba (Olympic skier).

Alec (223) Form of **Alexander.** Alec Baldwin, Sir Alec Guinness (actors). **Alek.**

Alejandro (204) Spanish form of **Alexander.** Alejandro Pena (baseball player), Alejandro Portes (sociologist). **Alexandro.**

Alex (64) Form of **Alexander.** Alex Karras (football player and actor), Alex Keaton (character on TV series *Family Ties*). **Alix, Allex.**

Alexander (33) Greek "defender of men." Alexander III (general and king of ancient Macedonia), Alexander Graham Bell (inventor of the telephone). **Alasdair, Alec, Alejandro, Alejo, Alejos, Aleksandr, Alessandro, Alex, Alexandre, Alistair, Alizondo, Sandor, Sandro, Sandy.**

Alexis (410) Greek "defender, helper." Alexis de Tocqueville (French author).

Alfonso (378) Spanish form of Old German *Adolfuns*, "noble and eager," from *athal* [noble] + *funs* [ready]; a Spanish royal name brought to Spain by the Visigoths. Alfonso Ortiz (Native American anthropologist). **Afonso, Alfonsin, Alonsa, Alonzo, Alphonse, Alphonso, Foncho, Fonso, Loncho, Poncho.**

Alfred (367) Old English *Aelfred*, from *aelf* [elf] + *raed* [counsel]. Alfred Eisenstaedt (photographer), Alfred Hitchcock (film director). **Al, Alf, Alfie, Alfredo, Avery, Elfred, Fred.**

Alfredo (479) Spanish and Italian form of **Alfred**. Alfredo Kraus (operatic tenor), Alfredo Pirri (sculptor).

Alonzo (363) Spanish form of **Alfonso**. Alonzo G. Decker (cofounder, Black & Decker Co.). **Alonso, Alonza, Lon, Lonnie.**

Alvin (336) Old English *Aethelwine*, "noble friend," from *aethel* [noble] + *wine* [friend] or *Aelfwine* from *aelf* [elf] + *wine* [friend]. Alvin Ailey (choreographer), Sergeant Alvin York (WW I hero). **Aluin, Alvino, Alvy, Alwyn, Aylwin, Elvin, Elwin.**

Amir (450) Arabic "ruler, tribal chief." Amir Naderi (film director). **Ameer.**

Amos (466) Hebrew "burden" or "burden carrier." Amos Oz (novelist).

Andre (134) French form of **Andrew**. Andre Agassi (tennis player), Andre Gide (author).

Andres (272) Spanish form of **Andrew**. Andres Segovia (classical guitarist).

Andrew (7) Greek *andreas* or *andreios*, "man, manly, strong." Andrew Jackson (seventh U.S. president), Andrew Lloyd Webber (composer). **Anders, Andre, Andreas, Andres, Andy, Drew.**

Andy (322) Form of **Andrew**. Andy Rooney (TV commentator), Andy Warhol (artist).

Angel (229) Form of **Angelo**. Angel Cordero (jockey).

Angelo (304) Italian form of Greek *angelos*, "a messenger"; translation of a Hebrew word meaning "a messenger of God." **Andel, Angel, Angelos, Aniol, Gelo, Lito.**

Anthony (22) Latin *Antonius*, a Roman family name of unknown meaning. Anthony Hopkins (actor), Anthony Kennedy (U.S. Supreme Court justice). **Antal, Antek, Antoine, Anton, Antonin, Antonio, Antony, Toncho, Tony.**

Antoine (177) French form of **Anthony**. Antoine de Saint-Exupery (author and aviator). **Antjuan, Antuan, Antwan, Antwann, Antwoine, Antwon.**

Antonio (91) Spanish and Italian form of **Anthony**. Antonio Vivaldi (composer). **Tonio.**

Ariel (491) Hebrew "lion of God." Ariel
Sharon (Israeli politician).

Armando (379) Spanish form of **Herman:**
Old German *Harimann*, from *harja* [army] +
mann [man]. Armando Acosta (film director),
Armand Assante (actor). **Armand, Armondo.**

Arthur (197) Possibly Latin *Artorius*, a
family name; also possibly Celtic *artos*, "a
bear," or Irish *art*, "a stone." Arthur Ashe
(tennis player), Arthur Miller (playwright).
Art, Artero, Artie, Arturo.

Ashton (327) Old English place name, "ash
tree farm." Ashton Phelps, Jr. (newspaper
publisher).

Austin (51) Middle English form of Latin
Augustus, "venerable." Sir Austen
Chamberlain (1925 Nobel Prize winner for
peace). **Austen.**

Avery (384) Norman French form of **Alfred.**
Avery Brooks (actor), Avery Schreiber
(comedian).

Barry (256) Irish *bearach*, "spear." Barry
Goldwater (politician), Barry Levinson
(filmmaker). **Barrie.**

Beau (240) French "handsome"; also short
form of **Beauregard,** "handsome look." Beau
Bridges (actor), Beau Williams (gospel
singer). **Bo, Boe.**

Ben (428) Usually a form of **Benedict,
Benjamin, Bennett,** or **Bernard;** also Scottish
beann, "peak," or Hebrew *ben,* "son of." Ben
Shahn (artist), Ben Vereen (entertainer).

Benjamin (34) Hebrew "son of the south" or
"son of the right hand." Benjamin Franklin
(statesman and inventor), Benjamin Spock
(pediatrician). **Ben, Benjy, Benny, Binyamin,
Venyamin, Yemin.**

Bernard (343) Old German *Berinhard,*
"brave as a bear," from *berin* [a bear] + *hard*
[stern]. Bernard Malamud (author), Bernard
Shaw (TV newscaster). **Barnard, Barney,
Ben, Berardo, Bernal, Bernard, Bernardo,
Berndt, Bernhard, Bernie, Nardo.**

Billy (172) Form of **William.** Billy Graham
(evangelist), Billy Joel (musician). **Billie.**

Blaine (293) Scots Gaelic *Blaan,* "yellow."
Blaine Peterson (hockey player). **Blaan,
Blain, Blane, Blayne.**

Blair (499) Celtic "plains," a Scottish place.
Blair Kiel (football player), Blair Underwood
(actor). **Blaire, Blayre.**

Blake (81) Old English *blac,* "pale" or
"shining"; also Old English *blaec,* "black,
dark." Blake Edwards (film producer and
director). **Blayke.**

Bobby (160) Form of **Robert.** Bobby Darin
(singer and actor), Bobby Fischer (chess
champion). **Bobbie.**

Brad (317) Old English *brad*, "broad"; also shortened form of **Bradley** or **Bradford.** Brad Davis (actor). **Bradd.**

Braden (246) Irish Gaelic *Bradain*, "salmon." **Bradon, Brayden.**

Bradley (56) Old English "broad meadow." Bradley Brookshire (harpsichordist), Bradley Googins (sociologist). **Brad, Bradlee, Bradlie, Bradly.**

Brady (263) Irish Gaelic *Bradaigh*, perhaps "spirited"; also Old English *brad eage*, "broad eye" (nickname) or *brad eg*, "broad island" (place name). **Bradie.**

Brandon (19) English place name, "hill covered with broom," though in Ireland sometimes a form of **Brendan.** Brandon Cruz (actor), Brandon Tartikoff (TV executive). **Branden, Brandin, Brandyn.**

Brant (457) Old Norse *Brandr*, "sword, firebrand." Brant Calkin (environmentalist). **Brandt.**

Brendan (119) Irish Gaelic *Breanainn*, itself a form of Old Welsh *breenhin*, "prince." Brendan Behan (playwright), Brendan Shanahan (hockey player). **Brenden, Brendon.**

Brennan (275) Irish Gaelic *Braonain*, form of *braon*, "drop of water, tear." **Brenan, Brennen, Brennon, Brennyn, Brenon.**

Brent (108) Old English "burnt," as in a burned place or field; or Celtic "high." Brent Scowcroft (presidential adviser), Brent Spiner (actor).

Brenton (347) Old English place name, "Bryni's homestead." Brenton Schlender (business reporter). **Brenten.**

Brett (71) Old French *bret, breton,* "a person from Brittany." Bret Harte (novelist), Bret Saberhagen (baseball player). **Bret, Brit.**

Brian (23) Probably from Celtic *Brigonos,* "high, noble." Brian Dennehy (actor), Brian Mulroney (prime minister of Canada). **Briand, Brion, Bryan, Bryant, Bryon.**

Brock (211) Old English *brocc,* "badger," or *broc,* "brook." **Broc.**

Brody (478) Scots Gaelic *brothach,* "muddy place," or Slavic *brod,* "ford." **Brodie.**

Bruce (202) French *Braose,* a forest in France; introduced into England at time of the Norman Conquest (A.D. 1066) but soon associated with Scotland because a Norman of this name settled there. Bruce Springsteen (rock musician), Bruce Willis (actor). **Brewis, Brucie.**

Bryant (198) Form of **Brian.** Bryant Gumbel (TV personality). **Briant.**

Bryce (120) Form of **Brice,** Celtic name of fifth century French saint, uncertain meaning. Bryce Courtenay (novelist), Brice Marden (artist). **Brice, Brizio.**

Bryson (402) Middle English "son of Brice." **Brycen, Brysen.**

Byron (251) Old English *byre,* "cow shed." Byron Dorgan (member of Congress), Byron White (U.S. Supreme Court justice). **Biron, Byrom.**

Cade (446) Old English *Cada,* "lump," or Middle English *cade,* "pet." Cade Newman (nutritionist). **Kade.**

Caleb (66) Hebrew *kalebh,* "dog." Caleb Finch (neurobiologist). **Cale, Calob, Cayleb, Kaleb, Kaylob.**

Calvin (139) Latin *calvus,* "bald"; surname of John Calvin, the founder of Calvinism in the sixteenth century. Calvin (character in comic strip *Calvin & Hobbes*), Calvin Coolidge (30th U.S. president). **Cal, Calvino.**

Cameron (58) Scots Gaelic *cambron,* "crooked hill," or *camshron,* "bent nose." Cameron Mackintosh (theatrical producer), Cameron Mitchell (actor). **Cam, Camron, Kameron.**

Carl (103) Form of German **Karl,** itself a variation of **Charles.** Carl Jung (psychoanalyst), Carl Sandburg (poet). **Karl.**

Carlos (106) Spanish form of **Charles.**
Carlos Montoya (guitarist), Carlos Salinas de
Gortari (president of Mexico).

Carlton (325) Form of **Charlton:** Old English
ceorlatun, "town of freemen," from *ceorl*
[freeman] + *tun* [town]. Carlton Caves
(physicist), Carlton Fisk (baseball player).
Karlton.

Carson (357) Scottish surname, several
possible meanings include "marsh-dweller."
Karsen, Karson.

Carter (429) Middle English "cart driver."
Carter J. Eckert (historian).

Cary (437) Middle English *Kari,* perhaps
"pleasant stream," or Irish Gaelic *O Ciardha,*
"son of the dark one." Cary Elwes, Cary
Grant (actors). **Carey, Kary.**

Casey (74) Irish Gaelic *Cathasach,*
"watchful." Casey Blake (historian), Casey
Stengel (baseball manager). **Casy, Kacey,
Kasey.**

Cedric (265) First appeared in *Ivanhoe* by
Sir Walter Scott, who may have mistaken it
for *Cerdic,* the mythical founder of West
Saxony; *Cerdic* may derive from Welsh
Caradawg, "amiable." Cedric Garland
(epidemiologist), Cedric Hardwicke (actor).
Ced, Cedrick, Rick, Sedrick.

Cesar (413) Spanish form of Latin *Caesarius*, possibly "hairy child." Cesar Chavez (labor activist), Cesar Romero (actor). **Cezar, Sesar.**

Chad (76) Old English *Ceadda*, name of a seventh century bishop, possibly based on Welsh *cad*, "battle." Chad Everett (actor), Chad Mitchell (singer). **Chadd.**

Chadwick (400) English place name, "Saint Chad's village." Chadwick Alger (political scientist).

Chance (233) Nineteenth century American short form of **Chauncey,** English surname from a French place name (though meaning of word "chance" obviously affects modern use). **Chanse, Chantz.**

Chandler (351) Old French *chandelier*, "candle maker." Chandler Davidson (political scientist).

Charles (40) Old German *carl*, "a man," through Latin *Carolus*. Charles, Prince of Wales; Charles Dickens (author). **Carl, Carlino, Carlo, Carlos, Carol, Carroll, Charlie, Chaz, Chuck, Karel, Karl, Karol, Karoly.**

Charlie (395) form of **Charles.** Charlie Chaplin (comedian). **Charley.**

Chase (96) Old French *chaceur*, "hunter." Chase Gioberti (character on TV series *Falcon Crest*). **Chace, Chaise, Chayse.**

Chaz (323) Form of **Charles.** Chaz Brenchley (novelist). **Chas, Chazz.**

Chris (389) Form of **Christopher** or **Christian.** Kris Kristofferson (actor and musician), Chris Sarandon (actor). **Kris.**

Christian (65) Greek *christos,* "anointed one," through Latin *Christianus,* "Christian," and French *Christiane.* Christian Laettner (basketball player). **Carsten, Chretien, Chris, Cristino, Karstin, Krikszte, Kristian, Kristo, Zan.**

Christopher (2) Greek *Kristophoros,* "Christ bearing" (one who carries Christ in his heart); through Latin *Christopherus.* Christopher Columbus (navigator); Christopher Reeve (actor). **Chris, Christofer, Christoph, Christophe, Christy, Cristobal, Cristofer, Cristoforo, Kester, Kit, Kristofel, Kristofer, Kristoffer, Kristopher, Krzysztof, Risto.**

Clarence (312) English, from title of the Duke of Clarence, itself from Clare, a place name, perhaps from Celtic "lukewarm stream." Clarence Clemmons (saxophonist), Clarence Thomas (U.S. Supreme Court justice). **Clare, Clarencio, Claron.**

Clay (362) Old English *claeg,* "clay." Clay Cole (entertainer), Clay Jacobson (inventor of the jet ski). **Klay.**

Clayton (127) English place name, "place with good clay for making pottery." Clayton Yeutter (U.S. secretary of agriculture). **Klayton.**

Clifford (280) Old English "ford at a cliff." Cliff Clavin (character from TV series *Cheers*), Clifford Odets (playwright). **Cliff.**

Clifton (424) Old English "place on a cliff." Clifton Davis, Clifton Webb (actors). **Cliffton.**

Clint (326) Form of **Clinton**. Clint Black (country singer), Clint Eastwood (actor and director). ˙

Clinton (147) English place name, "hill town," from Old Norse *klettr* [hill] + Old English *tun* [town]. **Clint, Klinton.**

Cody (27) Irish Gaelic *Mac Oda,* perhaps "son of Odo [Old German 'riches']." American use honors Buffalo Bill Cody. Cody Carlson (football player). **Kody.**

Colby (149) Old Norse/Old English "Cole's farm," English place name. Colby Rodowsky (children's author). **Colbie, Kolby.**

Cole (216) Old English *col,* "coal-black," or form of **Nicholas**. Cole Porter (composer and lyricist).

Colin (93) Scots Gaelic *cailean,* "youth" or "cadet"; or a medieval form of **Nicholas**. Colin Blakely (actor), Colin Powell (U.S. Army general). **Colan, Collin.**

Colton (101) Old English *colt-tun*, "town where colts are bred"; also "Cola's or Koli's town." **Coleton, Kolton.**

Connor (141) Irish Gaelic *Conchobar*, "wolf-lover." Conor Cruise O'Brien (Irish statesman and author). **Conn, Conner, Conor.**

Corbin (303) Old French *corbin*, "raven." Corbin Bernsen (actor). **Corben, Corbyn, Korbin.**

Corey (32) Old Norse *Kori* or Irish Gaelic *Comhraide*, both of unknown meaning. Corey Feldman (actor), Corey Pavin (golfer). **Corie, Corry, Cory, Korey, Korry, Kory.**

Cornelius (361) Roman clan name, probably from Latin *cornu*, "horn." Cornelius Bennett (football player), Cornelius Vanderbilt (railroad magnate). **Cornelious.**

Cortez (419) Spanish surname, perhaps meaning "dweller at a royal court." **Cortes, Kortez.**

Coty (298) French surname from Breton *coz ty*, "old house," or Norman French *coteau*, "small slope." **Koty.**

Courtney (237) Middle English *de Curtenay*, from *Courtenay*, French place name, "short one's manor." **Cortney, Kortney.**

Craig (102) Celtic *creag*, "crag" (rock). Craig Morton (football player), Craig Wilson (water polo player). **Cragg, Kraig.**

Curtis (97) Old French *corteis*, "courteous" or "educated." Curtis Strange (golfer). **Curt, Kurtis.**

Dakota (144) Name of a Native American nation. Dakota Jackson (furniture designer). **Dakotah.**

Dale (250) Old English *dael*, "valley, hollow." Dale Bumpers (U.S. senator), Dale Ellis (basketball player). **Dayle.**

Dallas (299) Old English *dalhous*, "house in the valley"; also Scottish place name "resting place." Dallas Green (baseball manager).

Dallin (438) Old English *Dallinges*, "Pride's people"; English place name. Dallin Oakes (lawyer and Mormon church leader). **Dalin, Dallan, Dallen, Dallon.**

Dalton (150) Old English *daltun*, "valley farm." Dalton Hilliard (football player).

Damian (159) Form of **Damien,** Greek *damazein*, "to tame." Father Damien de Veuster (missionary to Hawaiian lepers). **Dameon, Damien, Damion.**

Damon (273) Classical Greek form of **Damian.** Damon Runyon (author), Damon Wayans (actor). **Damen, Daymon.**

Dane (239) Old English *denu*, "valley," Middle English "a Dane," or French *dein*, "honorable." Dana Carvey (comedian), Dane Clark (actor). **Dana, Dain, Daine, Dayne.**

Daniel (12) Hebrew "God is my judge."
Daniel Boone (pioneer), Daniel Webster
(statesman). **Dan, Danek, Danilo, Danny,
Deiniol, Taneli.**

Danny (192) Form of **Daniel.** Danny DeVito,
Danny Glover (actors). **Dannie.**

Darius (113) Persian "he who upholds the
good." Darius Milhaud (composer). **Darias,
Darious, Darrius, Derrius.**

Darnell (328) Middle English *Darnall*,
"hidden nook"; or Old French *darnel*, a plant
thought to produce giddiness. Darnell
Hawkins (sociologist). **Darnel.**

Darren (111) Form of Irish Gaelic *Dubhdara*,
uncertain meaning, though "black oak" is an
educated inference. Darren McGavin (actor).
Daren, Darin, Darrin, Darron, Derron.

Darrion (215) Modern blend of **Damian** and
Darren, or from *Darien*, Panamanian place
name. Darian Hagan (football player).
Darian, Darien, Darion, Darrian, Derrian.

Darryl (99) Middle English *deAyrel*, "from
Airelle," a town in northern France. Darryl
Strawberry (baseball player). **Dairell, Darl,
Darrel, Darrell, Daryle, Daryl, Derrell.**

David (8) Hebrew *Dodavehu*, perhaps
"darling or beloved of God"; originally a
lullaby word. David Bowie (musician), David
Souter (U.S. Supreme Court justice). **Dai,
Dako, Dave, Davis, Davy, Dewey, Taavi.**

Dean (271) Latin *decanus*, "chief of ten," through Middle English *deen*, "dean"; also Old English *dene*, "valley." Dean Jones (actor), Dean Rusk (U.S. secretary of state). **Deane, Dene.**

DeAndre (209) African-American creation, *De* + **Andre**. **D'Andre, Deondre, Diondre.**

DeAngelo (332) Form of *DiAngelo*, Italian "son of Angelo." **D'Angelo, DiAngelo.**

DeJuan (421) African-American creation, *De* + **Juan**. **D'Juan, Dajuan, Dawon, Dewaun, Dewon, D'Won.**

DeMarcus (341) African-American creation, *De* + **Marcus**. **Damarcus, Demarkis, Demarkus, D'Marcus.**

Demetrius (191) Greek *Demetrios*, "belonging to Demeter, goddess of fertility." Demetrius A. Klein (choreographer). **Dametrius, Damitrius, Demetrice, Demetrious, Demetris, Demitrios, Demitrius, Dimitri, Dimitrios, Dimitrius.**

Dennis (126) French *Denys* from Latin *Dionysius* and Greek *Dionysos*, the god of wine. Dennis Conner (yachtsman), Dennis Eckersley (baseball player). **Den, Denes, Denis, Denys, Dion, Dionigi, Dionis, Dionisio, Dionizy, Dwight.**

Denzel (387) From *Denzell*, a Cornish place name, uncertain meaning. Denzel Washington (actor and director). **Denzell, Denzil.**

Deon (313) Short form of *Dionysus*, name of the Greek god of wine. Dion (rock musician). **Dion.**

Deontae (270) African-American creation, blend of **Deon** and **Donte. D'Ante, Deante, Deonte, Diante, Diontay, Dionte.**

Derek (38) Dutch *Diederick* or *Direk* from Old German *Theodoric*, "people-power." Derek Bok (president of Harvard University), Derrick Coleman (basketball player). **Darric, Darrick, Deric, Derick, Derik, Derrick, Deryk, Dirk.**

DeRon (480) African-American creation, *De* + **Ron. Daron, Daronn, Deronne.**

DeShawn (372) African-American creation, *De* + **Shawn. Dashaun, Dashawn, DeSean, DeShaun, D'Shawn.**

Desmond (259) Irish Gaelic *Desmumhnach*, "man from South Munster." Desmond Morris (British zoologist and author). **Des, Dezmond.**

Devin (62) Irish Gaelic *Daimine*, "fawn," or Old French *devin*, "excellent." Devon is also the name of a county in southwestern England. Devin Carroll (entomologist), Devon White (baseball player). **Devinn, Devon, Devyn.**

Dexter (319) Old English *deghstre*, "dyer." Dexter Busse, Dexter Carter (football players).

Diego (436) Form of Spanish **Santiago,** "Saint James." Diego Maradona (soccer player), Diego Rivera (Mexican artist).

Dominic (117) Latin *dominicus,* "of the Lord," often referred to the Lord's day, Sunday, and given to children born that day. Dom DeLuise (comedian). **Dom, Domenico, Domingo, Dominick, Dominik, Dominique, Domonkos, Mingo, Nick.**

Dominique (163) French form of **Dominic.** Dominique Lapierre (author and philanthropist), Dominique Wilkins (basketball star). **Domineek, Domonique.**

Don (487) Form of **Donald.** Don Johnson (actor), Don McLean (musician).

Donald (79) Scots Gaelic *Domhnall* and Old Irish *Domnall,* "world mighty." Donald Sutherland (actor), Donald Trump (real-estate developer). **Don, Donal, Donaldo, Donnell, Donnie.**

Donnie (369) Form of **Donald.** Donny Osmond, Donnie Wahlberg (singers). **Donny.**

Donovan (245) Irish Gaelic *Donnduban,* "dark brown swarthy person." Donovan Leitch (Scottish musician popularly known by first name only). **Donavan, Donavon.**

Dontavius (467) African-American creation, blend of **Donte** and **Octavius. Dantavius, Dontavious.**

Donte (169) Italian *durante*, "lasting."
Closely associated with Dante Alighieri,
author of *The Divine Comedy*. Dante Bichette
(baseball player). **Dantae, Dantay, Dante,
Dontay, Dontey, Durante.**

Dorian (447) Greek "man from Doris"
(central Greece). Dorian Gray (title character
in Oscar Wilde novel). **Dorien, Dorion.**

Douglas (88) Gaelic *dubhglas*, "dark blue";
a common Celtic river name and later the
name of a great Scots clan. Douglas Adams
(author), Douglas MacArthur (U.S. Army
general). **Doug, Dougal, Douglass, Duggie.**

Drew (130) Old German *Drogo*, "to carry";
introduced into England at time of the
Norman Conquest (A.D. 1066) in French form
Drues; also a form of **Andrew.** Drew Hill
(football player), Drew Westen
(psychologist).

Dustin (50) English place name, "dusty
place." Dustin Hoffman (actor). **Dustan,
Dusten, Duston, Dusty, Dustyn.**

Dwayne (195) Form of **Duane:** Irish Gaelic
Dubhain, form of *dubh*, "black." Duane Eddy
(band leader), Dwayne Woodruff (football
player). **DeWayne, Duane, Dwain, Dwaine.**

Dwight (388) Probably Middle English *Diot*,
form of *Dionysus* (see **Dennis**). Dwight
Eisenhower (34th U.S. president), Dwight
Gooden (baseball player).

Dylan (63) Welsh "of the sea." Dylan was the god of the ocean waves. Dylan Thomas (poet). **Dillan, Dillon, Dyllan, Dylon.**

Earl (316) Old English *eorl*, "noble man or warrior"; one of the oldest noble titles. Earl Monroe (basketball player), Earl Warren (U.S. Supreme Court justice). **Earle, Erl, Erle, Irl.**

Eddie (208) Form of names beginning with *Ed-*. Eddie Albert (actor), Eddie Murphy (actor and comedian). **Eddy.**

Edgar (374) Old English *Eadgar*, from *ead* [wealth] + *gar* [spear]. Edgar Cayce (psychic), Edgar Allen Poe (poet). **Ed, Eddie, Edgardo.**

Eduardo (308) Spanish form of **Edward.** Eduardo Matos Moctezuma (archaeologist).

Edward (73) Old English *Eadweard,* from *ead* [wealth] + *weard* [guardian]. Edward Albee (playwright), Edward Kennedy (U.S. senator). **Duarte, Ed, Eddie, Edouard, Eduardo, Edvard, Edvardas, Ned, Ted.**

Edwin (225) Old English *Eadwine*, "rich friend," from *ead* [wealth] + *wine* [friend]. Edwin Bailey (football player), Edwin Arlington Robinson (poet). **Ed, Eddie, Eduin, Eduino, Edwyn, Ned, Ted.**

Eli (305) Hebrew "height"; also a form of **Elijah** or **Elisha.** Eli Wallach (actor), Eli Whitney (inventor). **Ely.**

Elijah (214) Hebrew "Yahweh is my God."
Elijah Cook, Jr. (actor), Elie Wiesel (author).
Elia, Elias, Elie.

Elliott (186) Middle English *Elyot,* form of
both **Elias** and Old English *Aelfweald,* "elf
rules." Elliott Gould (actor), Elliott
Richardson (cabinet member and
ambassador). **Eliot, Eliott, Elliot.**

Emilio (449) Spanish form of Latin
Aemilius, a Roman family name that may
mean "rival." Emilio Ambasz (architect),
Emilio Estevez (actor). **Emelio, Emil,
Emiliano, Emilius.**

Emmanuel (181) Hebrew "God is with us."
Emmanuel Lewis (actor). **Emanuel,
Immanuel, Manuel.**

Enrique (397) Spanish form of **Henry.**
Enrique Batiz (conductor).

Eric (25) Old Norse, possibly from *ei*
[always] + *rikr* [ruler]. Eric Clapton
(musician), Eric Heiden (Olympic speed
skater). **Erich, Erick, Ericus, Erik, Rick.**

Ernest (248) German *Ernst,* "vigor,
earnestness." Ernest Borgnine (actor),
Ernest Hemingway (novelist). **Arnost,
Earnest, Ernesto, Ernie, Erno, Ernst.**

Ervin (485) Form of **Irving:** Scottish place
name meaning "green river." Earvin "Magic"
Johnson (basketball player). **Earvin, Irvin.**

Esteban (484) Spanish form of **Steven.**
Esteban Krotz (anthropologist), Esteban
Torres (member of Congress). **Estevan.**

Ethan (55) Hebrew "strength, permanence,
firmness." Ethan Allen (early American
patriot), Ethan Coen (film director).

Eugene (252) Greek *eugenios,* "well-born."
Gene Kelly (dancer, choreographer, and film
director), Eugene O'Neill (playwright).
**Eugen, Eugenio, Gene, Geno, Jeno, Owen,
Yevgeni.**

Evan (69) From *Ifan,* Welsh form of **John.**
Evan Hunter (author). **Ev, Evin, Yvaine.**

Everett (439) Old German *Eburhart,* "strong
as a boar," from *ebur* [wild boar] + *hard*
[strong]. Everett M. Dirksen (U.S. senator),
C. Everett Koop (U.S. surgeon General). **Ev,
Everard, Evy.**

Ezekiel (426) Hebrew "the strength of God."
Zeke Mowatt (football player). **Esequiel,
Ezequiel, Zeke.**

Fabian (420) Form of *Fabius,* a Roman
family name from Latin *faba,* "bean." Fabian
Forte (singer popularly known by first name
only). **Fabien.**

Felix (440) Latin *felix,* "happy." Felix
Frankfurter (U.S. Supreme Court justice),
Felix Jose (baseball player). **Feel, Felice.**

Fernando (365) Spanish form of
Ferdinand: Gothic, from *fard* [journey] +
nand [ready]. Ferdinand Magellen
(navigator), Fernando Valenzuela (baseball
player). **Ferando, Ferdi, Fernan, Hernando.**

Forrest (306) Old English "forest" or
"forester." Forrest Sawyer (TV journalist).
Forest.

Francis (235) Latin *Franciscus,* "a Frank."
Francis of Assisi (Italian saint and founder of
Franciscans), Francis Ford Coppola (film
director). **Ferenc, Fran, Francisco, Franco,
Francois, Frang, Frank, Franz, Franzisko.**

Francisco (234) Spanish form of **Francis.**
Francisco J. Ayala (biologist), Francisco
Toledo (painter). **Paco, Pancho.**

Frank (112) Old French *franc,* "free man";
also form of **Francis.** Frank Sinatra (singer),
Frank Lloyd Wright (architect).

Franklin (279) Middle English *frankeleyn,*
"a free landowner." Franklin Pierce (14th
U.S. president), Franklin Delano Roosevelt
(32nd U.S. president). **Franklyn.**

Fred (443) Form of **Frederick.** Fred Astaire
(dancer and actor), Fred Savage (actor).

Freddy (409) Form of **Frederick.** Freddy
Fender (country singer), Freddie Mercury
(musician). **Freddie.**

Frederick (157) Old German "peaceful ruler." Frederick Douglass (African-American speaker and writer), Frederic March (actor), **Drick, Federico, Fred, Freddy, Frederic, Fredric, Fredrick, Fredrik, Friedrich, Fritz, Ric.**

Gabriel (109) Hebrew "man of God," an angel who appeared to Daniel in the Old Testament and Mary in the New Testament. Gabriel Faure (French composer), Gabriel García Márquez (author). **Gabe, Gabrial.**

Gage (294) Old Norman French *gauge*, "fixed measure," used for someone who checked official weights and measures in medieval times. Gage White (photographer). **Gaige.**

Garrett (77) Middle English form of **Gerard** or **Gerald.** Garrett Limbrick (football player), Garrett Morris (actor and comedian). **Garret, Gary, Gerrit.**

Gary (98) Middle English form of **Garrett.** Gary Cooper (actor), Gary Player (golfer). **Garrie, Garry.**

Gavin (274) Scottish form of Welsh *Gwalchgwyn*, "white hawk." Gavin Langmuir (historian), Gavin McLeod (actor). **Gav, Gaven, Gawain.**

George (84) Greek *georgos*, "farmer." George Bush (41st U.S. president), George Bernard Shaw (playwright). **Geordie, Georg, Georges,**

Giorgio, Gyorgy, Jerzy, Jorge, Jorgen, Jurgen, Yorick, Yuri.

Gerald (151) Old German *Gairovald,* "spear ruler," from *ger* [spear] + *vald* [rule]. Gerald Ford (38th U.S. president). **Garrett, Geraldo, Gerhold, Gerolt, Giraldo, Jarrett, Jerald, Jerold, Jerrell, Jerrold, Jerry.**

Gerard (469) Old German *Gairhard,* "spear-brave," from *ger* [spear] + *hardu* [hard]. Gerard Depardieu (actor), Gerard Manley Hopkins (poet). **Garrett, Gellert, Gerardo, Gerhard, Gerrit, Girard, Jarrett, Jerry.**

Gerardo (495) Italian and Spanish form of **Gerard.** Gerardo (Hispanic rap musician).

Gilbert (462) Old German *Gisilbert,* from *gisil* [pledge] + *berht* [bright]. Gil Hodges (baseball player), Gilbert Morris (novelist). **Gil, Gilberto.**

Giovanni (227) Italian form of **John.** Giovanni Agnelli (Italian carmaker).

Glenn (196) Celtic *gleann,* "wooded valley, dale, glen." Glen Campbell (musician), Glenn Gould (pianist). **Glen, Glyn, Glynn.**

Gordon (386) Uncertain origin, but may come from a French place name, *Gourdon;* or from Celtic *gor* [spacious] + *din* [fort]. Gordon Lightfoot (singer), Gordon Parks (photographer and filmmaker). **Gordie, Gordy.**

Graham (335) Old English *Grantham* from *granta* [gravel] + *ham* [home or village] or *Granta's ham*. Graham Greene (novelist), Graham Kerr (chef). **Graeme, Grahame, Gram.**

Grant (154) Old French *grant*, "grand, tall." Grant Tinker (TV producer), Grant Wood (artist).

Grayson (494) Middle English *Grayveson*, "son of the grieve, or steward." **Greyson.**

Gregory (53) Greek *gregorios*, "watchful." Gregory Hines (actor and dancer), Gregory Peck (actor). **Gergely, Goyo, Greg, Gregoire, Gregor, Gregorio, Grigori, Grzegorz.**

Hakeem (404) Arabic, "most wise," from one of the 99 traditional names of Allah. Hakeem (formerly Akeem) Olajuwon (basketball player). **Haakim, Hakiem, Hakim.**

Harold (282) Old English *hereweald* from *here* [army] + *weald* [power]; also Old Norse *Harivald*. Hal Holbrook (actor), Harold Pinter (playwright). **Hal, Haral, Harald, Haroldo, Harry, Herald.**

Harrison (242) Middle English *Herryson*, "son of **Henry**." Harrison Ford (actor), Harrison Salisbury (journalist).

Harry (321) Form of **Harold** or **Henry**. Harry Blackmun (U.S. Supreme Court justice), Harry S Truman (33rd U.S. president). **Hal.**

Hassan (482) Arabic *hasan*, "good, beautiful." King Hassan II of Morocco, Hassan Sabra (journalist). **Hasan.**

Hayden (307) Old English *heg denu*, "hay valley," English place name; or Irish Gaelic *Eideain*, "armor." Hayden Carruth (poet), Hayden Herrera (art historian). **Haden, Haydon.**

Heath (401) Old English *haeth*, "land covered with shrubs." Heath Barkley (character on TV series *The Big Valley*), Heath Dillard (historian).

Hector (289) Greek *hektor*, "restrainer." Hector Berlioz (composer), Hector Elizondo (actor). **Ector, Ettore, Heck, Hektor.**

Henry (148) Old German *Haimirich*, from *haimi* [home] + *ric* [ruler]. Henry Fonda (actor), Henry Ford (industrialist). **Anrai, Enrico, Enrique, Hank, Harry, Heinrich, Heinz, Hendrik, Henri, Henrico.**

Herbert (430) Old German *Hariberct*, from *harja* [army] + *berhta* [bright]. Herbert Hoover (31st U.S. president), Herbert Lom (actor). **Bert, Bertie, Erberto, Hebert, Herb, Herbie, Heriberto.**

Howard (310) Uncertain origin but may be Old German *Huguard*, "protector of the soul," from *hugu* [heart] + *vardu* [guard]. Howard Fast (author), Howard Hughes (industrialist, aviator, and movie producer). **Howdy, Howie, Ward.**

Hunter (207) Middle English *huntere,* "huntsman." Hunter Thompson (journalist).

Ian (67) Scottish form of **John.** Ian Fleming (writer), Ian Holm (actor). **Ean, Iain.**

Isaac (124) Hebrew "laughter." Isaac Asimov (author), Sir Isaac Newton (mathematician). **Ike, Isak, Isacco, Izaak, Yitzhak.**

Isaiah (161) Hebrew "Yahweh is salvation." Isiah Thomas (basketball player). **Isaias, Isiah, Izaiah.**

Israel (412) Hebrew *Yisrael,* "may God reign" or "wrestling with God." Israel Kaplan (educator). **Iser, Yisrael.**

Ivan (260) Russian form of **John.** Ivan Albright (American painter), Ivan Lendl (tennis player).

Jace (338) Form of **Jason.** Jace Alexander (actor). **Jase, Jayce.**

Jack (156) Form of **John,** from Middle English *Jankin, Jackin.* Jack Jones (singer), Jack Nicholson (actor). **Jackie.**

Jackie (459) Form of **Jack.** Jackie Robinson (baseball player). **Jacky.**

Jackson (266) Middle English *Jakson,* "son of Jack." Jackson Browne (musician), Jackson Pollock (painter). **Jaxon.**

Jacob (24) Hebrew *Ya'aqob'el*, "may God protect," later interpreted as "supplanter." Jacob Javits (U.S. senator), Jacobo Timerman (author). **Giacobbe, Jacobo, Jacques, Jake, Jakie, Jakob, James, Yakov.**

Jaime (315) Spanish form of **James**. Jaime Escalante (math teacher, subject of film *Stand and Deliver*).

Jake (142) Form of **Jacob** and **James**. Jake La Motta (prizefighter, subject of film *Raging Bull*).

Jamal (171) Arabic "handsomeness." Jamaal Wilkes (basketball player). **Jamaal, Jamahl, Jamal, Jamall, Jamaul, Jhamal.**

Jamar (324) African-American creation, blend of **Jamal** and **Lamar. Jamarr, Jemar, Jimar.**

Jamel (394) Form of **Jamal** or **Jamil.** Jamel Chelly (geneticist). **Jamell, Jemel.**

James (5) English form of **Jacob;** came to England from Late Latin *Iacomus* through Spanish *Jayme.* James Madison (4th U.S. president), James Earl Jones (actor). **Diego, Giacomo, Iago, Jacques, Jago, Jaime, Jake, Jamie, Jay, Jaymes, Jim, Jimmy, Santiago.**

Jameson (368) Middle English *Jamesson*, "son of **James.**" Jameson Parker (actor). **Jamieson, Jamison.**

Jamie (180) Form of **James,** especially common in Scotland. Jamie Farr (actor).

Jamil (405) Arabic "handsome." Jamil M. Abun-Nasr (historian). **Jameel, Jhamil.**

Jared (48) Akkadian "servant." Jared Diamond (ornithologist and linguist), Jared Sparks (historian). **Jarod, Jarred, Jarrod, Jerad, Jered, Jerod, Jerrad, Jerrid, Jerrod.**

Jaron (244) In most cases a modern creation blending sounds of **Jared** and **Darren;** however, **Gerin, Jerin,** and **Geron** were Old French short forms of **Gerald, Gerard, Gervaise,** or **Gerontius** (Greek "old man"). Jaron Lanier (inventor of virtual reality computer programs). **Gerron, Jaren, Jarin, Jarren, Jarron, Jeron, Jerron.**

Jarrett (219) Middle English form of **Gerald** or **Gerard.** Jarrett Hedborg (interior decorator). **Jarett, Jarret, Jerett, Jerrett.**

Jarvis (290) English form of Old French *Gervaise,* itself from Old German *ger* [spear] + *vass* [servant]. Jarvis Brown (baseball player), Jarvis Williams (football player).

Jason (46) Greek "the healer"; used in New Testament times as a Greek form of **Joshua.** Jason (mythological figure), Jason Robards (actor). **Jace, Jacen, Jaison, Jasen, Jay, Jaysen, Jayson.**

Javier (258) Form of **Xavier.** Javier Perez de Cuellar (secretary-general of the U.N.).

Javon (411) African-American creation, *Ja-* + *-von.* Javon Jackson (jazz musician). **Javonne, Jevon.**

Jay (155) Old French *jaí,* "bluejay," from Latin *gaius,* "rejoiced in"; also form of **James, Jason,** and other names beginning with *J.* Jay Leno (comedian and talk-show host).

Jean (460) French form of **John.** Jean Genet (playwright), Jean-Jacques Rousseau (philosopher).

Jeffrey (37) Form of **Geoffrey:** Old German *Gaufrid* "peaceful land," or *Walahfrid* from "peaceful traveller," or *Gisfrid* "pledge of peace"; Middle English *Geffrey* from Old French *Geoffroi.* Popular form in U.S. is Jeffrey; in England, Geoffrey. Jeff Bridges, Jeffrey Hunter (actors). **Jeff, Jeffery, Jeffry.**

Jeremiah (125) Hebrew "may God raise up, exalt." Jeremiah Healy (mystery writer), Jeremiah Johnson (title character in movie). **Geremia, Jeremias, Jeremy, Jerry, Yirmeyah.**

Jeremy (41) English form of **Jeremiah.** Jeremy Bentham (philosopher), Jeremy Irons (actor). **Jeremie, Jeromy.**

Jermaine (254) Form of French *Germain,* "a German." Jermaine Jackson (singer), Jermain Loguen (anti-slavery crusader). **Jermain, Jermane.**

Jerome (253) Greek *Hieronymos*, "holy name." Jerome Kern (composer), Jerome Robbins (choreographer). **Geronimo, Girolamo, Jeroen, Jeronimo, Jerry.**

Jerrell (288) Modern blend of **Gerald** and **Darryl.** Jerel Rosati (political scientist). **Gerrell, Jarell, Jarrel, Jarrell, Jerel, Jerell, Jerrel, Jerryl.**

Jerry (129) Form of **Jeremiah, Gerald, Gerard,** or **Jerome.** Jerry Brown (governor of California), Jerry Lewis (comedian). **Gerry, Jere.**

Jesse (47) Hebrew "God exists." Jesse Jackson (civil rights leader), Jesse James (Old West desperado). **Jess, Jessie, Yishai.**

Jesus (213) Greek form of **Joshua,** "God saves." Jesus Alou (baseball player). **Hesus, Jesu.**

Jimmy (145) Form of **James.** Jimmy Carter (39th U.S. president), Jimmy Smits (actor).

Joe (287) Form of **Joseph.** Joe DiMaggio (baseball player), Joe Louis (prizefighter).

Joel (100) Hebrew "the Lord is God." Joel Coen (film director), Joel Grey (actor). **Yoel.**

Joey (375) Form of **Joseph.** Joey Bishop (comedian).

John (9) Hebrew *Johanan,* "the Lord has favored" or "the Lord is gracious." John (one of the Twelve Apostles), John F. Kennedy (35th U.S. president). **Evan, Giovanni, Hans, Ian, Ivan, Jack, Jan, Jean, Jens, Joao, Jock, Johann, Johnny, Jon, Juan, Sean, Shane, Shawn, Yochanan.**

Johnny (123) Form of **John.** Johnny Carson (TV personality), Johnny Cash (country singer). **Johnnie.**

Jonathan (16) Hebrew "God has given" or "God's gift." Jonathan Swift (author), Jonathan Winters (comedian). **Johnathan, Johnathon, Jon, Jonathen, Jonathon, Jonnathan, Jonothan.**

Jordan (28) Hebrew *yardan* "to descend," the river name. Jordan Knight (singer). **Jorden, Jordin, Jordon, Jordyn.**

Jorge (187) Spanish form of **George.** Jorge Bell (baseball player), Jorge Tacla (artist).

Jose (78) Spanish form of **Joseph.** Jose Canseco (baseball player), Jose Carreras (operatic tenor).

Joseph (15) Hebrew "the Lord added [children]." Joseph Conrad (author), Joseph Papp (producer and director). **Giuseppe, Joe, Joey, Jose, Josef, Josephito, Jozef, Osip, Yosef, Yussuf, Yusuf.**

Joshua (3) Hebrew "God saves." Joshua Logan (film director), Joshua Slocum (first person to sail around the world solo). **Giosue, Jesus, Josh, Joshuah, Josue, Yehoshua.**

Josiah (301) Hebrew "God heals." Josiah Willard Gibbs (physicist), Josiah Wedgewood (founded company that makes china). **Josh, Josia, Josias, Si.**

Josue (455) Spanish form of **Joshua.**

Juan (110) Spanish form of **John.** Juan Berenguer (baseball player), Juan Carlos (King of Spain).

Julian (118) Latin *Julianus* from **Julius.** Julian Bond (civil rights activist), Julian Lennon (musician). **Giuliano, Jule, Julianus, Juliao, Julien, Julio, Julion.**

Julio (337) Spanish form of **Julian.** Julio Iglesias (singer).

Julius (331) Roman clan name, probably from *Jovilios,* "descended from Jove" (Jupiter). Julius Ceasar (Roman general), Julius Erving (basketball player). **Jules, Julian, Yul.**

Justin (6) Latin *justus,* "the just." Justin Henry (actor), Justin Kaplan (author). **Giustino, Iestyn, Justino, Justo.**

Kadeem (433) English form of Arabic *Khadeem,* "servant," or *Qadeem,* "ancient." Kadeem Hardison (actor). **Kadim.**

Kalin (366) Origin unknown; perhaps a modern creation based on **Cale** or **Caleb**. **Calen, Calin, Caylon, Kaelan, Kalen.**

Kareem (417) Arabic "noble." Kareem Abdul-Jabbar (basketball player). **Karim, Karime.**

Keaton (390) English surname of uncertain meaning. **Keiton, Keyton.**

Keegan (344) Irish Gaelic *Mac Aodhagain*, "son of *Aeducan*," itself a form of *Aed*, "fire." **Keagan, Keegen, Kegan.**

Keenan (278) Irish Gaelic *Cianain*, form of *Cian*, "enduring." Keenan Ivory Wayans (actor and comedian), Keenan Wynn (actor). **Keenen, Keenon, Kenan.**

Keith (82) Scottish place name; origin and meaning unknown but may come from Gaelic "the wind" or "the forest." Keith Hernandez (baseball player), Keith Richards (rock musician).

Kellen (454) Perhaps from a German place name meaning "swamp." Kellen Winslow (football player). **Kellan.**

Kelly (311) Irish Gaelic *cellach*, "bright-headed" or *ceallach*, "strife." Kelly Gruber (baseball player), Kelly Slater (surfer).

Kelvin (291) Name of a Scottish river, uncertain meaning. Kelvin Bryant (football player).

Kendall (238) English place name, "valley of the River Kent." Kendall Walton (art critic). **Kendal, Kendell, Kendle.**

Kendrick (297) Welsh *Cynwrig*, from *cyn* [chief] + *gwr* [hero]. Kendrick Smithyman (poet). **Kendric.**

Kenneth (52) Scots Gaelic *Coinneach*, "handsome" or *Cinaed*, "fire-sprung." Kenneth Clark (psychologist). **Ken, Kenny.**

Kenny (425) Form of **Kenneth.** Kenny Rogers (singer and actor), Kenny Stabler (football player).

Kent (452) Name of a county in southeastern England, perhaps Celtic "coast." Kent Berridge (brain scientist), Kent Taylor (actor).

Keon (431) African-American creation, probably a masculine form of **Kiana** (see list of popular girls' names). **Keyon, Kion.**

Kerry (380) "*Ciar's* people," Irish place name. *Ciar* itself meant "black." Kerry W. Buckley (biographer).

Kevin (29) Irish *Caomhan*, "loved" or *Caemgen*, "beautiful birth." Kevin Arnold (main character on TV series *The Wonder Years*), Kevin Costner (actor). **Keven.**

Khalil (435) Arabic "companion, friend." Kahlil Gibran (poet). **Kahlil, Kalil, Khaleel.**

Khiry (432) Origin unclear, but probably an African-American form of *Khayri*, Arabic "benevolent." Khiry Abdul-Samad (singer). **Khiri, Kiry.**

Kiefer (474) German "barrel-maker" or "pine tree." Kiefer Sutherland (actor). **Keefer.**

Kirk (296) Scottish form of Old English *ciric*, "church." Kirk Douglas (actor), Kirk Gibson (baseball player). **Kirke.**

Kurt (226) Form of **Konrad:** Old German *Conrad*, "bold counsel." Kurt Russell (actor), Kurt Vonnegut (author). **Curt.**

Kwame (461) Akan (Ghana) "born on Saturday." Kwame Holman (TV reporter). **Kwami, Quame.**

Kyle (21) Scots Gaelic "narrow strait." Kyle Abbott (baseball player), Kyle MacLachlan (actor). **Kile, Ky.**

Kyler (434) Dutch *Cuyler*, "archer," or German *Keiler*, "wild boar." **Cuyler, Kylor.**

Lamar (286) French *la mare*, "the pond." Lamar Alexander (U.S. secretary of education). **Lamarr.**

Lamont (465) Old French *le mont*, "the mountain"; or Scots Gaelic *laomainn*, from Old Norse *logmadr*, "lawman." **Lammond, Lamond, Monty.**

Lance (164) Form of Norman French *lancelot,* "the servant." Lance Armstrong (bicyclist), Lance Johnson (baseball player).

Landon (276) Probably form of **Langdon,** Old English "long Hill." Landon Turner (basketball player).

Lane (382) English "path" or "roadway." Lane Bradford (actor). **Laine, Layne.**

Larry (121) Form of **Lawrence.** Larry Bird (basketball player), Larry McMurtry (author). **Larrie.**

Lawrence (158) Latin *laurentius* from *laurus,* "laurel." Sir Laurence Olivier (actor), Lawrence Taylor (football player). **Larry, Lars, Laurance, Laurence, Laurens, Laurent, Lawrance, Loren, Lorenz, Lorenzo.**

Lee (173) Old English *leah,* "meadow"; also form of **Leland, Leo,** or **Leroy.** Lee DeForest (inventor), Lee Majors (actor). **Lea, Leigh.**

Leo (442) Latin "lion." Leo Durocher (baseball manager), Leo Sayer (singer). **Lee, Leon, Leone, Leos.**

Leon (330) Greek form of **Leo.** Leon Redbone, Leon Russell (musicians).

Leonard (257) Old German "lion hard." Leonard Bernstein (composer), Leonard Nimoy (actor and director). **Len, Lenard, Lennard, Lennart, Lennie, Leonardo, Leonhard, Lowenhard.**

Leonardo (492) Italian, Spanish, and Portuguese form of **Leonard.** Leonardo da Vinci (artist, sculptor, and inventor).

Leroy (364) Old French *le roi,* "the king." LeRoy Burrell (sprinter), Leroy Jenkins (composer). **Lee, Leeroy, LeRoi, Roy.**

Leslie (468) Scottish clan name of uncertain origin, possible meanings include "garden by the pool" and "court of hollies." Leslie Nielsen (actor). **Les, Lesley, Lessie.**

Lester (481) Form of *Leicester,* from *Ligore* [a tribal name of uncertain meaning] + *cester* [from Latin *castra,* "city"]. Lester Archambeau (football player), Lester Thurow (economist). **Les.**

Levi (133) Hebrew "joined, attached." Levi Strauss (jeans manufacturer). **Levon, Levy.**

Lloyd (448) Welsh *Llwyd,* "gray" or "holy." Lloyd Bentsen (U.S. senator), Lloyd Bridges (actor). **Loyd.**

Logan (92) Scots Gaelic "little hollow," Scottish place name. Logan Jackson (activist for the homeless). **Logen.**

Lonnie (383) Form of **Alonzo.** Lonnie Coleman (author), Lonnie Mack (jazz guitarist). **Lonny.**

Lorenzo (339) Spanish and Italian form of **Lawrence.** Lorenzo Lamas (actor), Lorenzo White (football player). **Loren, Renzo.**

Louis (138) Old German *Hludwig,* "famous
warrior"; Latin *Ludovicus* became French
Louis, spelled **Lewis** in Great Britain. Louis
Armstrong (musician), Louis L'amour
(Western author). **Lew, Lewie, Lodewick,
Lou, Ludwig, Luigi, Luis.**

Lucas (95) Latin *Lucanus,* "man from
Lucania," a place in southern Italy, uncertain
meaning. Lucas Samaras (artist). **Lukas.**

Luis (114) Spanish form of **Louis.** Luis
Alvarez (physicist), Luis Aparacio (baseball
player). **Luiz.**

Luke (104) Greek *Loukas,* "a person from
Lucania." Luke Perry (actor), Luke
Skywalker (character in movie *Star Wars*).

Mackenzie (370) Scottish Gaelic "son of
Kenneth." Mackenzie King (prime minister
of Canada). **MacKensie, McKenzie.**

Malcolm (201) Gaelic *maol Columb,*
"servant of Saint Columb" from Latin
columbia, "dove." Malcolm Forbes
(publisher), Malcolm X (civil rights leader).
Mal, Malcom.

Malik (352) Arabic "king." Malik al-Shabazz
(Arabic name of Malcolm X). **Maleek, Malek,
Malique.**

Manuel (255) Spanish form of **Emmanuel.**
Manuel Lujan (U.S. secretary of the interior),
Manuel Ocampo (artist).

Marcel (444) French form of *Marcellus*, Latin form of **Marcus.** Marcel Marceau (pantomimist), Marcel Proust (author). **Marcell.**

Marco (348) Italian form of **Mark.** Marco Livingstone (art historian), Marco Polo (Italian traveler and explorer).

Marcos (416) Spanish form of **Mark.** Marcos Dantus (chemist).

Marcus (68) Form of **Mark.** Marcus Garvey (African-American political activist). **Markus.**

Mario (168) Italian form of Latin *Marius*, Roman clan name, probably related to Mars, the god of war. Mario Cuomo (governor), Mario Puzo (novelist).

Mark (45) Latin *Marcus*, a Roman forename probably derived from *Mars*, god of war. Mark Lenzi (Olympic diver), Mark Twain (author). **Marc, Marco, Marcos, Marcus, Marek, Marko.**

Marlon (356) Probably a form of *Marlin*, French form of *Merlin*, the Latin form of *Myrddin*, Welsh "sea hill." Marlon Brando (actor), Marlon Jones (football player). **Marlin, Marlen.**

Marquis (182) Medieval Latin *marchensis*, "count of a borderland," an English and French title of nobility. Marquis Childs (author). **Markwis, Marques.**

Marquise (385) Title of a female marquis, but used by African Americans as a boy's name. **Markweese, Marquece, Marqueese.**

Marshall (228) Old French *marshal*, "horse groom" and later "a leader of men." Marshall Field (merchant), Marshall McLuhan (author). **Marshal.**

Martin (153) Latin *Martinus*, form of *Martius*, "of Mars." Martin Luther King, Jr. (civil rights leader), Martin Scorsese (film director). **Mart, Martino, Martyn.**

Marvin (247) Old English *maerwine* from *maer* [famous] + *wine* [friend]; or form of Old Welsh *Merfyn*, ancient royal name, uncertain meaning. Marvin Gaye (singer), Marvin Hamlisch (songwriter). **Marv, Marve, Marven, Mervyn, Merwyn.**

Mason (167) Old French *masson*, "a stonecutter." Mason Williams (composer and musician). **Mace, Sonnie.**

Matthew (4) Hebrew *matisyahu*, "gift of the Lord." Matthew (one of the Twelve Apostles), Matthew Broderick (actor). **Mateo, Mateusz, Mathew, Mathieu, Mats, Matt, Matteo, Matti.**

Maurice (179) Latin *Maurus*, "a Moor." Maurice Chevalier (entertainer), Maurice Sendak (illustrator). **Mauricio, Maurits, Maurizio, Mauro, Maury, Moritz, Morris.**

Max (170) Form of Latin *maximus*, "the greatest," or **Maxwell.** Max Lerner (columnist), Max Planck (physicist). **Maxie, Maxim, Maximo, Maxy.**

Maxwell (184) Scottish place name, "Maccus's well." Maxwell Anderson (playwright). **Max.**

Melvin (267) Perhaps masculine form of **Malvina,** invented by Scottish poet James Macpherson in the 1700s or, less likely, from Irish Gaelic *maoillmhin*, "gentle chief." Melvin Belli (attorney), Melvin Stewart (Olympic swimmer). **Mel, Melvyn, Vinny.**

Micah (190) Hebrew "Who is like Yahweh?" Micah L. Sifry (journalist). **Mica, Mika, Myka.**

Michael (1) Hebrew "Who is like the Lord?" Michael Jackson (singer), Michael Jordan (basketball player). **Micheal, Mickel, Micky, Miguel, Mike, Mikhail, Mikko, Misha, Mitchell.**

Miguel (175) Spanish form of **Michael.** Miguel de Cervantes Saavedra (author of *Don Quixote*). **Migel.**

Miles (185) Old German *milo* possibly from Slavic *milu*, "merciful," or Latin *miles*, "soldier." Miles Davis (jazz trumpeter), Myles Standish (English colonist in America). **Milan, Milo, Myles.**

Mitchell (80) Form of **Michael.** Mitchell Kapor (software designer, founder of Lotus Development Co.), Mitch Williams (baseball player). **Mitch.**

Mohammad (349) Arabic "praiseworthy." The name of Islam's prophet has become the most common male name in the world. Muhammad Ali (champion prizefighter). **Mohamad, Mohammed, Muhammad.**

Morgan (222) Welsh either *mor* [sea] or *mawr* [great] + *can* [bright]. Morgan Freeman (actor). **Morgen.**

Nathan (43) Hebrew "the given." Nathan Hale (American Revolutionary hero). **Nat, Natan, Nate, Nathen, Nathon, Natty.**

Nathaniel (72) Hebrew "God has given." Nathaniel Branden (author), Nathaniel Hawthorne (novelist). **Nat018aneal, Nataniel, Nathanael.**

Neil (188) Irish Gaelic *Niall,* uncertain meaning, perhaps "passionate," "cloud," or "chief." Neil Armstrong (astronaut and first man on the moon), Neil Diamond (singer). **Neal, Neale, Nels, Nial, Niall, Niel, Niels, Nigel, Nils.**

Nelson (302) "Son of Neil." Nelson Algren (author), Nelson Rockefeller (41st U.S. vice-president).

Nicholas (10) Greek *nikolaos* from *nike*
[victory] + *laos* [people] through Latin
Nicolaus. Nicholas Brady (U.S. secretary of
the treasury), Nick Nolte (actor). **Claus, Cole,
Colin, Klaus, Miklos, Nichol, Nicholaus,
Nicholis, Nick, Nickalas, Nicklaus, Nickolas,
Nicky, Nico, Nicolao, Nicolas, Nicolaus,
Nicolo, Niklas, Nikolai, Nikolaos, Nikolas,
Nikolaus.**

Nico (464) Greek, Italian, and Dutch form of
Nicholas. Nico Charisse (dancer and
choreographer). **Niko.**

Noah (206) Hebrew "rest" or "wandering."
Noah (Biblical patriarch), Noah Webster
(lexicographer). **Noe.**

Noel (463) Latin *natalis*, "birth," through Old
French *noel* or *nowel;* traditionally used as a
name for children born on Christmas Day.
Sir Noel Coward (playwright). **Nowel,
Nowell.**

Nolan (318) Irish Gaelic *Nuallain,* from
nuall, "shout." Nolan Ryan (baseball player).
Noland, Nolen.

Norman (391) Old English "North man."
Norman Rockwell (artist), Norman
Schwarzkopf (U.S. Army general). **Norm,
Normand, Normen.**

Octavius (475) Roman family name from
Latin *octavus*, "eighth." **Octavious.**

Oliver (393) Uncertain meaning, perhaps Old German *Alfihar*, "elf-host"; or Old French "olive tree." Oliver Wendell Holmes (U.S. Supreme Court justice), Oliver Stone (film director). **Noll, Nolly, Olivier, Olivo, Ollie.**

Omar (249) Arabic "thriving" or Hebrew "speaker." Omar Bradley (U.S. Army general), Omar Sharif (actor). **Omer.**

Orlando (353) Spanish form of **Roland.** Orlando Cepeda (baseball player), Orlando Figes (historian).

Oscar (261) Old English *osgar* from *os* [god] + *gar* [spear]. Oscar de la Hoya (boxer), Oscar Hammerstein (dramatist). **Oskar.**

Owen (399) Welsh form of **Eugene.** Owen Gingerich (astrophysicist). **Ewan, Ewen, Owayne.**

Pablo (498) Spanish form of **Paul.** Pablo Casals (conductor), Pablo Picasso (painter).

Parker (241) Old English "gamekeeper." Parker Stevenson (actor). **Park.**

Patrick (44) Latin *patricius*, "member of the nobility." Saint Patrick (patron saint of Ireland), Patrick Henry (American patriot). **Paddy, Padraig, Pat, Patric, Patrice, Patricio, Patrizio, Patsy.**

Paul (57) Latin *paulus*, "small." Paul McCartney (composer and singer), Paul

Newman (actor and director). **Paavo, Pablo, Pal, Paolo, Pavel, Pavlo, Pol.**

Pedro (333) Spanish form of **Peter.** Pedro Almodovar (film director), Pedro Guerrero (baseball player).

Perry (396) Old English *pyrige,* "pear tree." Perry Como (singer), Perry Ellis (fashion designer).

Peter (86) Greek *petros,* "rock." Peter (one of the Twelve Apostles), Peter O'Toole (actor). **Peder, Pedro, Per, Pierce, Piero, Pierre, Piers, Pietro, Pyotr.**

Phillip (59) Greek *philippos,* "horse lover." Philip (one of the Twelve Apostles), Phil Collins (singer). **Felipe, Filip, Flip, Phil, Philip, Philippe, Pip.**

Pierre (493) French form of **Peter.** Pierre Renoir (French impressionist painter), Pierre Trudeau (prime minister of Canada).

Preston (162) Old English "priest's town." Preston Foster (actor), Preston Sturges (director and screenwriter).

Quentin (264) Latin "the fifth." Quentin Blake (illustrator), Quentin Burdick (U.S. senator). **Quenten, Quenton, Quinn, Quintin, Quinton, Quintus.**

Quincy (472) French "fifth son's place." Quincy Jones (musician), Quincy Watts (runner). **Quin, Quincey.**

Quinn (398) Irish Gaelic *O Cuinn,* "grandson of Conn," perhaps meaning "wise leader"; also form of **Quentin** or **Quincy.** Quinn Martin (TV producer), Quinn Redeker (actor). **Quin.**

Quinton (178) Form of **Quentin,** or English place name, "queen's manor." Quintin Dailey (basketball player), Quintin Smith (football player). **Quinnton, Quintan, Quinten, Quintin, Quintyn.**

Rafael (205) Form of **Raphael:** Hebrew "God cures" or "God has healed." Rafael Kubelik (conductor), Rafael Palmiero (baseball player), Raphael Sanzio (artist). **Rafe, Raffaello.**

Raheem (470) Arabic *rahim,* "compassionate." **Rahiem, Rahim.**

Rakeem (490) Arabic *raaqim,* "writer, recorder." Rakim (rap musician). **Rakim, Rhakeem.**

Ralph (414) Old German *Radulf,* from *rat* [counsel] + *wulf* [wolf], through Norman French *Raulf.* Ralph Abernathy (civil rights leader), Ralph Waldo Emerson (poet). **Rafe, Ralf, Raoul, Raul.**

Ramon (342) Spanish form of **Raymond.** Ramon Martinez (baseball player), Ramon Myers (historian).

Randall (136) Form of **Randolf** or
Randolph: Old English *Randwulf* from *rand*
[shield-rim] + *wulf* [wolf]. Randall
Cunningham (football player), Randall
Jarrell (poet). **Rand, Randal, Randall,
Randell, Randey, Randi, Randie, Randle,
Randy.**

Randy (122) Form of **Randall** and **Randolf.**
Randy Quaid (actor), Randy White
(basketball player).

Rashad (236) Arabic "good spiritual
guidance." **Rashaad, Rashod.**

Rasheed (488) Arabic "rightly guided,
mature." Rasheed Araeen (artist). **Rashid.**

Raul (377) Spanish form of **Ralph.** Raul de
Molina (photographer), Raul Julia (actor).

Ray (354) Form of **Raymond;** also French
rei, "king." Ray Bradbury (author), Ray
Charles (vocalist).

Raymond (94) Old German *Raginmund* from
ragan [advice] + *mund* [protector]. Raymond
Burr (actor), Raymond Carver (poet).
**Raimondo, Raimundo, Ramon, Ray,
Redmond, Reinmund.**

Reese (456) Welsh *Rhys*, "ardor." Reese
Cleghorn (journalist, media critic). **Reece,
Rees, Rhys.**

Reginald (200) Old English *Regenweald*, *ragan* [advice] + *weald* [power]. Reginald F. Lewis (first African-American to head a Fortune 500 corporation). **Reinaldo, Renaut, Reynaldo, Reynold, Ronald.**

Reid (355) Old English *read*, also English *hreod*, "reed." Reid R. Keays (geologist), Reid Nagle (financial analyst). **Reade, Rede, Reed.**

Rene (500) French form of Latin *Renatus*, "reborn." Rene Descartes (philosopher), Rene Dubos (environmentalist).

Ricardo (194) Spanish form of **Richard.** Ricardo Legoretta (architect), Ricardo Montalban (actor). **Rico.**

Richard (39) Old English "strong ruler." Richard Burton (actor), Richard Pryor (actor and comedian). **Dick, Hick, Reico, Ricardo, Rich, Rick, Ricky, Riik, Rikard, Ritchie.**

Rick (477) Form of **Richard.** Rick Moranis (actor), Rick Nelson (singer).

Ricky (135) Form of **Richard.** Ricky Skaggs (country singer). **Rickey, Rickie.**

Rico (458) Short form of **Ricardo.** Rico Labbe (football player), Rico Martinez (director).

Riley (221) Irish Gaelic *Raghailligh*, perhaps "valiant," or Middle English *Ryeley*, "rye field," a place name. Riley Smith (basketball player). **Reilly, Rylee, Ryley.**

Robert (14) Old English *Hreodberorht,* "shining in fame" from *hrothi* [fame] + *berhta* [bright]. Robert Frost (poet), Robert Redford (actor). **Bert, Bob, Bobby, Dob, Rab, Rob, Robbie, Roberto, Robin, Rupert, Ruprecht.**

Roberto (268) Spanish and Italian form of **Robert.** Roberto Alomar, Roberto Clemente (baseball players).

Roderick (269) Old German *Hrodric* from *hrothi* [fame] + *ric* [rule]. Roderick Phillips (historian), Roderick Tye (sculptor). **Gigo, Rod, Roddy, Roderich, Rodrigo, Rodrigues, Rurik, Ruy.**

Rodney (152) Old English "Hroda's Island." Rodney Dangerfield (comedian), Rod Laver (tennis player). **Rod, Roddy.**

Roger (174) Old English *Hrothgar* from *hrothi* [fame] + *gar* [spear]. Roger Mears (race car driver), Roger Moore (actor). **Dodge, Hodge, Rodge, Rodger, Rogelio, Rogerio, Rudiger, Ruggiero, Rutger.**

Roman (381) Latin *romanus,* "Roman." Roman Polanski (film director). **Romain, Romano**.

Ronald (83) Scottish form of **Reginald.** Ron Howard (actor and director), Ronald Reagan (40th U.S. president). **Renaldo, Ron, Ronaldo, Ronnie, Ronny.**

Ronnie (210) Form of **Aaron** or **Ronald.**
Ronnie Lott (football player), Ronnie Milsap
(singer and pianist). **Ronny.**

Rory (422) Irish Gaelic *Ruaidri,* "red king."
Rory Calhoun (actor), Rory Sparrow
(basketball player).

Ross (183) Form of Old German *Rozzo,*
"fame," or *hros,* "horse"; also Celtic *rhos,*
"moorland." Ross Martin (actor), Ross Perot
(entrepreneur and sometime presidential
candidate).

Roy (231) Gaelic *ruadh,* "red"; also Old
French *rei,* "king." Roy Romer (governor of
Colorado), Roy Scheider (actor). **Roi.**

Ruben (243) Form of **Reuben:** Hebrew
"behold a son." Ruben Blades (actor and
singer), Ruben Sierra (baseball player).
Reubin, Reuven, Rube.

Rudy (497) Form of **Rudolf:** Old German
Hrodwulf, from *hrod* [fame] + *wulf* [wolf].
Rudy Rucker (science fiction author), Rudy
Vallee (singer).

Russell (128) Old French *rous,* "red."
Russell Baker (humorist), Russell Long
(speedsailor). **Russ, Russel, Rusty.**

Ryan (13) Possibly Irish Gaelic *Rigan,* "little
king." Ryan O'Neal (actor), Ryan White
(AIDS activist). **Rian, Ryen, Ryon.**

Sam (403) Form of **Samuel** and **Samson.**
Sam Malone (main character on TV series
Cheers), Sam Walton (founder of Wal-Mart
stores).

Sammy (473) Form of **Samuel.** Sammy
Davis, Jr. (entertainer). **Sami.**

Samuel (49) Hebrew "name of God." Samuel
Beckett (playwright), Samuel Clemems
(author popularly known as Mark Twain).
Sam, Sammy, Samuele, Sawyl, Shmuel.

Scott (54) Old English "a Scotsman." Scott
Joplin (composer), Scott Turow (author).
Scot, Scotty.

Scotty (441) Form of **Scott.** Scottie Pippen
(basketball player), Scotty Schulhofer (race
horse trainer). **Scottie.**

Sean (26) Irish form of **John.** Sean Connery
(actor), Sean Penn (actor and director).
Seann, Shane, Shaun, Shawn.

Sebastian (285) Greek *sebastos*,
"venerable," through Latin *Sebastianus*,
"man from Sebastia." Sebastian Cabot
(actor), Sebastian Coe (runner). **Bastian, Seb,
Sebastiano, Sebastien, Sevastian.**

Sergio (309) Spanish and Italian form of
Sergius, a Roman clan name perhaps from
an Etruscan word for "servant." Sergio Leone
(film director), Sergio Mendes (musician).

Seth (89) Hebrew "set, appointed." Seth Morgan (novelist), Seth Thomas (clockmaker).

Shane (61) Form of **Sean**. Shane (title character in western movie), Shane Black (screenwriter). **Shain, Shayne.**

Shannon (314) Name of a river in Ireland, from a Celtic word meaning "the ancient god." Shannon Kelley (football player). **Shannen, Shanon.**

Shea (358) Irish Gaelic *segdae*, "hawk-like, stately." **Shae, Shay, Shaye.**

Shelby (427) Derivation same as girl's name **Shelby** (see list of popular girls' names). Shelby Foote (Civil War historian). **Shelbie.**

Sheldon (360) Old English *scylf-dun*, "flat-topped hill." Sheldon Cheney (author), Sheldon Glashow (physicist).

Sidney (453) Old English *sidenieg*, "wide, well-watered land," English place name. Sidney Lumet (director), Sidney Poitier (actor). **Sid, Sydney.**

Simon (376) Hebrew *shimeon*, "he heard," through Greek *Simon*, "snub nose" (a nickname). Simon Brett (mystery writer), Simon Rattle (conductor). **Jimeno, Semyon, Sim, Simao, Simeon, Szymon.**

Skyler (140) Modern form of *Schuyler,*
Dutch "scholar." Schuyler Colfax (17th U.S.
vice president). **Schuyler, Sky, Skylar,
Skylor.**

Spencer (87) Middle English "steward" or
"storekeeper." Spencer Tillman (football
player), Spencer Tracy (actor). **Spenser.**

Stacy (451) Medieval English form of
Eustace: Greek *eustakhios,* "fruitful." Stacy
Keach (actor). **Stacey.**

Stanley (262) Old English "stony meadow."
Stanley Kubrick (film producer and director),
Stan Musial (baseball player). **Stan,
Stanleigh, Stanly.**

Stefan (143) Scandinavian and German form
of **Steven.** Stefan Edberg (tennis player).
Steffan, Steffen, Stephan, Stephon.

Sterling (407) Old English *staerling,* "a
starling." Sterling Grey (humorist), Sterling
Hayden (actor). **Starling, Stirling.**

Steve (346) Form of **Steven.** Steve Martin
(actor and comedian), Steve McQueen (actor).

Steven (11) Form of **Stephen:** Greek
stephanos, "crown." Stephen King (author),
Steven Jobs and Steven Wozniak (cofounders,
Apple Computers, Inc.). **Esteban, Estefon,
Etienne, Istvan, Stefan, Stefano, Stepan,
Steve.**

Stuart (220) Form of **Stewart:** Old English *stigweard* from *stig* [hall] + *ward* [guard]. Stuart Whitman (actor). **Stew, Steward, Stu.**

Tanner (165) Old English *tannere,* "hide tanner." **Taner, Tanor.**

Tarik (489) Arabic "morning star." Tariq Ali (author). **Tareek, Tariq, Terik.**

Tavaris (406) Form of *Tavarez,* Spanish surname perhaps meaning "place of the hermit." Tavares (1970s rhythm and blues quintet). **Tavares, Tavarius, Tavarous, Tavarus.**

Taylor (60) Old French *tailleur,* "tailor." Taylor Hackford (film director). **Tayler.**

Terrance (107) Latin *Terentius,* a Roman family name, possibly related to *Terensis,* the goddess of milling grain. Terrance Dicks (children's author), Terence Stamp (actor). **Terance, Terence, Terencio, Terrence, Terris, Terry.**

Terrell (189) Middle English form of *Tirel.* Terrell Buckley (football player). **Tarell, Terel, Terell, Terrall, Terrel.**

Terron (408) Modern blend of **Terrance** and **Darren. Taran, Taron, Teron, Terran.**

Terry (132) Form of **Terrance** or Old French *Thierri,* a form of **Theodoric** (see **Derek**). Terry Bradshaw (football player).

Tevin (340) Probably a form of *Thevin*, French surname based on a medieval form of **Stephen.** Tevin Campbell (singer). **Teven, Tevon.**

Thaddeus (418) From Aramaic, unknown meaning. Thaddeus (one of the Twelve Apostles), Thaddeus O'Sullivan (film director). **Tad, Tadeo, Thad, Thaddaus, Thadeus.**

Theodore (203) Greek *Theodoros* from *theo* [god's] + *doros* [gift]. Theodore Geisel (Dr. Seuss), Theodore Roosevelt (26th U.S. president). **Fyodor, Ted, Teddy, Teodoro, Tewdwer, Theo, Theodor, Tivadar, Todaro, Todos**.

Thomas (30) Aramaic "twin." Thomas Edison (inventor), Thomas Jefferson (third U.S. president). **Tamhas, Tom, Tomas, Tommaso, Tommy, Tuomo.**

Timothy (31) Greek *Timotheos* from *time* [honor] + *theos* [god]. Timothy Dalton (actor), Timothy Egan (journalist). **Tim, Timmy, Timofei, Timothee, Timoteo.**

Tobias (476) Greek form of Hebrew *Tobiah*, "God is good." Tobias Wolff (author). **Tevye, Tobiasz, Toby, Tuvya.**

Toby (445) English form of **Tobias.** Toby Warson (munitions manufacturer). **Tobie.**

Todd (131) Old English *tod*, "fox." Todd Bridges (actor), Tod Sloan (jockey). **Tod.**

Tommy (230) Form of **Thomas.** Tommy John (baseball player), Tommy Tune (dancer).

Tony (137) Form of **Anthony.** Tony Bennett (singer), Tony Curtis (actor).

Tory (345) Middle English *Tori*, from Old Danish *Thorir*, "Thor, god of thunder." **Torey, Torrey, Torry.**

Tracy (371) Old French *Traci*, French place name for villages founded by Roman soldiers from Thrace in northern Greece. Tracy Murray (basketball player). **Tracey.**

Travis (42) Middle English *travers*, "toll," "toll collector." Travis McGee (fictional detective), Travis Tritt (country singer). **Traviss.**

Tremaine (423) Cornish place name, "farm with a stone monolith." Tramaine Hawkins (gospel singer). **Tramaine, Tremain, Tremayne.**

Trent (218) Name of English rivers and villages, perhaps from an ancient pre-Celtic word meaning "flooder." Trent Dimas (Olympic gymnast), Trent Lott (U.S. senator).

Trenton (199) Eighteenth-century American "*Trent's Town*," name of the city in New Jersey founded by William Trent. **Trenten.**

Trevor (70) Welsh *Trefor*, from *tref* [home] + *mor* [great or sea]. Trevor R. Bryce (archaeologist), Trevor Howard (actor). **Trefor, Trev, Trever.**

Trey (281) Latin *tres*, "three," originally a nickname for boys with Roman numeral III after their names. Trey Combs (sports fisherman). **Trae, Tray.**

Tristan (277) Form of **Tristram**: Celtic *drystan*, "tumult, loud noise." Tristan Platt (anthropologist), Tristan Rogers (actor). **Drystan, Tris, Tristem, Trystan.**

Troy (116) Middle English *Troie*, "from [French town of] Troyes"; or Irish Gaelic *troightheach*, "foot soldier"; or from ancient city made famous by the Trojan War. Troy Donohue (actor).

Tucker (359) Old English *tucian*, "to torment" through Middle English *touken*, "to stretch [cloth]." **Tuck.**

Ty (295) form of **Tyler, Tyree, Tyrone,** or **Tyson.** Ty Murray (rodeo champion).

Tyler (20) Old English *tygeler* or Old French *tieuleor*, both meaning "tile maker." Tyler Mathisen (financial reporter). **Tiler, Ty, Tylar, Tylor.**

Tyree (392) From *Tiree*, name of an island off the west coast of Scotland. Tyree Guyton (urban environmental artist). **Ty.**

Tyrel (329) Middle English *Tirel*, perhaps from Old French *tirer*, "stubborn." Tyrell Biggs (boxer). **Terrell, Tirrell, Tyrell, Tyrrell.**

Tyrone (217) Irish Gaelic "Owen's territory," and a county in Northern Ireland. Tyrone Corbin (basketball player), Tyrone Power (actor). **Ty, Tyron.**

Tyson (224) Old French *tison*, "firebrand." Tyson Anderson (philosopher). **Tison, Ty, Tycen, Tysen.**

Vernon (415) Common French place name, "alder-tree," brought to England by the Normans. Vernon Scannell (poet), Vernon Walters (U.S. representative to the United Nations). **Vern, Verne, Verney, Verny.**

Victor (115) Latin *victor*, "conqueror." Vic Damone (singer), Victor Hugo (author). **Toyano, Vic, Vick, Vico, Vik, Viktor, Viktoras, Vittore.**

Vincent (85) Latin *vincens*, "conquering." Vincent van Gogh (artist), Vince Lombardi (football coach). **Vicente, Vin, Vince, Vincente, Vinnie, Vinzenz, Wincenty.**

Wade (283) Old English *Wada*, "to go," name of a giant in ancient Germanic legends; or Middle English *wade*, "ford." Wade Boggs (baseball player), Wade Wilson (football player).

Walter (176) Old German *waldhar*, from *vald* [rule] + *harja* [people]. Walter Cronkite (TV newscaster), Walt Whitman (poet). **Gauthier, Gutierre, Walt, Wat, Watkin.**

Warren (300) Middle English *Warenne*, form of French *La Varenne*, place name meaning "game park." Warren Beatty (actor and director), Warren G. Harding (29th U.S. president).

Wayne (212) Old English *wain*, "wagon." Wayne Gretzky (hockey player), Wayne Newton (singer).

Wendell (483) Old Germanic "Wend" (a Slavonic tribe). Wendell Davis (football player), Wendell Willkie (1940 candidate for U.S. president). **Wendel, Wendle, Wendy.**

Wesley (90) Old English "west meadow." Wesley Person (basketball player), Wesley Snipes (actor). **Wes, Westley.**

Weston (284) Old English "west farm." Weston Dickson Fisler (baseball player). **Wes.**

Will (471) Form of **William.** Will Durant (historian), Will Rogers (comedian). **Wil.**

William (17) Old German *Wilahelm*, from *vilja* [will] + *helma* [helmet]. William J. Brennan, Jr. (U.S. Supreme Court justice), Bill Clinton (42nd U.S. president). **Bill, Billy, Guillermo, Liam, Wilhelm, Will, Willem, Willie.**

Willie (146) Form of **William.** Willie Mays (baseball player), Willie Nelson (singer). **Willi, Willy.**

Wyatt (350) Norman French *Wiot*, "little **Guy,**" from Old German *Wido*, "wide." Wyatt Earp (Old West lawman), Wyatt MacGaffey (historian).

Xavier (166) Basque *etcheberri*, "new house." Xavier McDaniel (basketball player). **Javier, Ksawery, Saverio, Xaver, Zavier.**

Zachariah (232) Hebrew "the Lord has remembered." Zachariah Chandler (founder of the Republican Party). **Zacarias, Zachary, Zechariah.**

Zachary (18) English form of **Zachariah.** Zachary Taylor (12th U.S. president). **Zach, Zacharey, Zachery, Zack, Zackary, Zackery, Zackry, Zakary, Zakery.**

Zane (320) From an American surname, origin unknown, but possibly from a Danish place name; an Americanized spelling of German *Zehn*, "ten" or "tenth"; or a form of Old English *Saewine*, "sea friend." Zane Grey (author), Zane Smith (baseball player).

Unusual
Boys' Names

Acton Old English *actun*, "town by the oaks."

Adlai Hebrew "God's justice." Adlai Stevenson (governor and presidential candidate).

Ahusaka Winnebago (Native American, Wisconsin) "strikes his wings."

Aidan Gaelic *Aedan*, form of *Aed*, "fire." Name of an Irish-born monk sent from Iona in Scotland to convert the then-heathen English to Christianity. Aidan Quinn (actor). **Aiden.**

Akihito Japanese "bright child." Emperor Akihito of Japan.

Akinyele Yoruba (Nigeria) "valor benefits this house."

Alasdair Gaelic form of **Alexander.** Alistair Cooke (journalist). **Alastair, Alastor, Alistair.**

Ali Arabic and Swahili "exalted, placed on the highest." **Aly.**

Amazu Ibo (Nigeria) "no one knows everything."

Anand Marathi (western India) "happiness."

Ara Armenian, ancient name of legendary Armenian king for whom Mount Ararat was named. Ara Parseghian (football coach).

Aristo Greek *aristos*, "best"; also form of **Aristotle** or **Aristophanes.**

Augustus Latin "magnificent." Augustus John (artist). **Augie, August, Augusto, Gus.**

Bailey Derivation same as girl's name **Bailey** (see list of popular girls' names). Bailey Millard (author). **Baile, Baily.**

Baliram Marathi (western India) "the strong one."

Barden Old English "barley valley." **Bard.**

Barnaby Greek *Barnabas*, "son of consolation," from Aramaic. Barnaby Jones (title character on TV series). **Barnabe, Barney.**

Basil Greek *basileios*, "royal." Basil Rathbone (actor). **Basilio, Vasili.**

Bjorn Scandinavian, Old Norse "bear." Bjorn Borg (tennis player). **Bjarne.**

Bomani Ngoni (Malawi) "warrior."

Brassal Irish Gaelic *bressal*, "brave or strong in conflict," name of an early king of Leinster. **Brazil, Brissal.**

Bronson Middle English *Brunson*, "son of the brown man." Bronson Pinchot (actor).

Burton Old English *burhton*, "from the fortress," from *burh* [fortified place] + *tun* [town]. Burt Reynolds (actor). **Bert, Burt.**

Chalmers Scottish form of Old French *chaumbre*, "private servant." Chalmers P. Wylie (member of Congress). **Chal.**

Clark Greek *kleros* and Latin *clericus*, "clerk, religious person, clergyman," through English *clerk*, "scholar" or "man of learning." Clark Gable (actor). **Clarke.**

Clement Latin *clemens*, "kind, gentle, mild, merciful." Clement Attlee (British prime minister). **Clem, Clemente, Kelemen, Klemens.**

Cleveland English place name, "land of cliffs, hilly district." Cleveland Amory (author and animal rights activist). **Cleve.**

Clive Old English *clif*, "cliff." Clive Barnes (critic). **Clyve.**

Cooper Middle English *couper*, "maker of barrels, vats, buckets."

Cyril Greek *kyrios*, "lord, master." Saint Cyril (inventor of Cyrillic alphabet used in Slavic countries), Cyril Ritchard (actor). **Cirilo, Cy, Cyrille, Kirill.**

Cyrus Persian *Kurush*, perhaps from *kuru*, "throne," through Greek *Kyros*, the great Persian king mentioned in the Old Testament. Cyrus Vance (U.S. secretary of state). **Cy.**

Darl Masculine form of **Darlene** or short form of **Darryl.**

Denver Old English *Denefaer*, "ford of the Danes," English place name.

Derry Short form of Irish **Dermot,** Gaelic *Diarmait*, name of an ancient hero considered the "greatest lover in Irish literature." Also Irish place name, perhaps meaning "oaks."

Doyle Irish Gaelic *O Dubhghaill*, "descendant of the dark stranger." Doyle McManus (journalist).

Drake Old English *Draca*, "dragon," or Middle English *drake*, "male duck." Drake Deming (astronomer).

Duncan Scottish form of Old Irish *dunecan*, "brown warrior." Duncan Hunter (member of Congress). **Dun, Dunn.**

Edmund Old English *Eadmund* from *ead* [wealth] + *mund* [protection]. Sir Edmund Hillary (mountaineer). **Ed, Edmond, Edmundo.**

Elton Old English "old farm"; or "Ella's village or farm." Elton John (musician). **Eldon.**

Elvis Perhaps a Welsh version of *Ailbhe*, an Irish-Gaelic name from Celtic *albho*, "white," though in the U.S. as likely to be a Southern creation blending sounds of **Alvin** and **Ellis.** Elvis Presley (singer and actor). **Alvis, El.**

Ezra Hebrew "help." Ezra Pound (poet). **Esdras.**

Fariji Swahili (East Africa) "consolation."

Farrell Irish Gaelic *fearghal*, "valorous," name of several medieval Irish kings. **Farall.**

Fletcher Old French *flechier*, "a maker of arrows." Fletcher Knebel (author). **Fletch.**

Galen Probably a Latin form of Greek *galene*, "calm." Galen Rowell (photographer).

Galway Irish place name, perhaps related to Celtic *gall*, "strange." Galway Kinnel (poet).

Garrick English form of French *Garrigue*, "grove of oaks." Garrick Utley (TV newscaster). **Garrik.**

Garth Old Norse *garthr*, "enclosure," through Middle English *garth*, related to "garden." Garth Brooks (country singer).

Giles Greek *aigidion*, "kid" (young goat), through Latin *Aegidius* and French *Gide*. Associated with soldiers because shields were made of goatskin. Giles Fowler (entertainment critic). **Egidio, Gil, Gilles, Gillis.**

Gintaras Lithuanian "amber," one of the national symbols of Lithuania.

Grover Old English "grove dweller." Grover Cleveland (22nd and 24th U.S. president). **Grove.**

Guion Old French *Guyon*, form of **Guy.** Guion Bluford, Jr. (first African-American astronaut).

Gunnar Old Norse *gunnarr*, "war." Gunnar Nelson (singer).

Guy Old German *wido*, either "wood" or "wide," through French *guy* and *guyon*. Guy Forget (tennis player). **Guido, Guyon, Wyatt.**

Hamisi Swahili (East Africa) "born on Thursday."

Harlan Old English *Harland*, "gray land." Harlan Ellison (science fiction author), Col. Harlan Sanders (founder of Kentucky Fried Chicken restaurants). **Harlen.**

Helaku Miwok (Native American, California) "sunny day."

Holden Old English *holedene*, "deep valley" from *hole* [hollow] + *dene* [valley]. Holden Caufield (central character in novel *The Catcher in the Rye*).

Houston Old English and Scottish "Hugh's town."

Hoyt Perhaps Irish "spirit, mind." Hoyt Axton (country singer). **Hoyte.**

Hugh Probably Old German *Hugu*, "heart, mind." Hugh Downs (TV journalist). **Hud, Huey, Hugo, Hutch, Huw, Ugo.**

Ikaika Hawaiian, "strength." Very popular in Hawaii in the 1980s.

Ira Hebrew "watchful" or Aramaic "stallion." Ira Gershwin (lyricist).

Jabari Swahili (East Africa) "brave."

Jaleel Form of Arabic *jalil*, "great, fine." Jaleel White (actor). **Jahleel, Jalil.**

Jelani Swahili (East Africa) "mighty."

Judson Middle English "son of Judd" (a form of **Jordan**). Judson Hale (editor). **Jud.**

Kaleo Hawaiian "the sound" or "the tune."

Kalmanu Miwok (Native American, California) "lightning striking a tree."

Kane Gaelic *Cathain*, "warrior" or Latin "battlefield" through *Caen*, French place name. **Kaine, Kayne.**

Keir Scots Gaelic *ciar*, "swarthy." Keir Dullea (actor).

Kirby Old English "church village" from *ciric* [church] + *by* [village]. Kirby Puckett (baseball player). **Kerby.**

Koit Estonian "dawn, daybreak."

Kyne Irish Gaelic *cadhan*, "wild goose," name of legendary hero who killed a monster with the aid of his magical hound.

Lachlan Scots Gaelic *Lachlann*, "fjordland, Norway." A very popular name in the 1980s in both Australia and Scotland.

Laird Scottish form of lord, in the sense of "landowner." Laird Cregar (actor).

Lal Sanskrit (India) "precious." Lal Shastri (prime minister of India).

Lanford Form of Old English *Langford*, "long ford," English place name. Lanford Wilson (playwright).

Lech Name of legendary ancestor of the Polish people. Lech Walesa (President of Poland).

Leeor Popular Israeli name, Hebrew "my light," often given to boys born on Hanukkah. **Lior.**

Lennox Scottish *leunaichs*, "place of elms," from Gaelic *leamhanach*. Lennox Lewis (boxer). **Lenox.**

Liam Irish short form of **William.** Liam Neeson (actor).

Lowell Norman French *lovel*, "wolf cub." Lowell Thomas (radio newscaster). **Lovell, Lowe.**

Lucian Latin *Lucianus*, probably from *lux*, "light." Lucian Freud (artist). **Lucien.**

Luther Old German *Liuther*, from *liut*, "people" + *heri*, "army." Luther Vandross (soul singer). **Lute.**

Lyle French *lisle*, "the island." Lyle Alzado (football player). **Lisle, Lyell.**

Lyman Possibly Old English "valley man." Lyman Lemnitzer (U.S. Army general).

Lyndon Old English "hill of linden trees." Lyndon Baines Johnson (36th U.S. president). **Lindon, Lyn.**

Madison Old English "son of Maude" or "son of Matthew." Madison Jones (author).

Mongeska Omaha (Native American, Nebraska) "white breast," referring to the white breast of deer. Native American name of Rodney Grant, actor who played Wind in His Hair in movie *Dances With Wolves.*

Monroe Gaelic *Rothach*, "man from Roe" (a river in Ireland). **Monro, Munro, Munroe.**

Montgomery French place name, "Gumric's hill." Gumric itself is an Old Germanic name from *gum* [man] + *ric* [powerful]. Montgomery Clift (actor). **Monte, Monty.**

Mostyn Welsh place name, "Fortress in a field"; currently popular in Wales.

Myron Greek "perfume." Myron Floren (accordionist). **Miron, Myreon.**

Neville French *Neuville*, "the new town."
Neville Marriner (conductor). **Nevil.**

Nevin Irish Gaelic *Naomhan*, form of *naomh*,
"holy," or *cnaimhim*, "bone." Nevin
Scrimshaw (nutritionist). **Nevan.**

Nijuga Winnebago (Native American,
Wisconsin) "rain man."

Nikhil Bengali (India, Bangladesh) "entire,
complete."

Obadiah Hebrew "servant of God." Obadiah
"Sky" Masterson (character in musical *Guys
and Dolls*).

Olaf Old Norse *Anulaibar* from *anu* [ancestor]
+ *leaibar* [remains]. Olaf Bar (baritone).

Orson Latin *ursus*, "bear," through French
Ourson. Orson Welles (actor and director).
Orso, Urso.

Osman Turkish form of Arabic *Uthmaan*,
"young crane." Osman (founder of the
Ottoman Empire). **Osmin, Othman.**

Otto Old German *audo*, "rich." Otto
Klemperer (conductor). **Odo, Otho, Oton,
Ottone.**

Peyton Old English "Paega's farm." **Payton.**

Prince Latin *princeps*, "the first, the leader."
Prince (musician).

Quaashie Ewe (Ghana) "born on Sunday."

Ravi Sanskrit (India) "the sun." Ravi Shankar (musician).

Rex Latin *rex*, "king." Rex Reed (critic). **Rey.**

Rhett Last name of a prominent South Carolina family, origin unknown but perhaps related to German *reth*, "reeds." Rhett Butler (major character in *Gone With the Wind*).

River Old French *rivere*, "river," from Latin *riparius*, "of the river bank." River Phoenix (actor).

Roden Irish Gaelic *Rodan*, "hearty, lively." Roden Noel (poet and literary critic).

Roland Old German *Hrodland*, "famous throughout the country," from *hrodi* [fame] + *landa* [land]. Roland (hero of French epic poem *The Song of Roland*). **Lorand, Orlando, Rolando, Roldan**.

Roosevelt Dutch "field of roses." Use as a first name honors Presidents Theodore and Franklin Delano Roosevelt. Roosevelt Grier (football player).

Rudyard Old English "pond with red carp," name of an English lake. Rudyard Kipling (poet). **Rudd, Rudy.**

Runako Shona (Zimbabwe) "handsome."

Rupert English form of **Ruprecht,** a German form of **Robert.** Rupert Brooke (poet).

Rutger Dutch form of **Roger.** Rutger Hauer (actor).

Sargent Latin *servient,* "server, attendant" through Old French *serjant.* Later became English *sergeant,* an army enlisted person's rank. Sargent Shriver (politician). **Sarge.**

Satoru Japanese "intelligence, understanding."

Sawyer Middle English *saghier,* "sawer, lumberman." Sawyer Brown (country music group).

Sherman Old English *scearramann,* "man who shears cloth or sheep." Sherman Minton (U.S. Supreme Court justice).

Shomari Swahili "forceful."

Sigmund Old German *sigumund* from *sigus* [victory] + *mund* [shield]. Sigmund Freud (founder of psychoanalysis). **Siegmund, Sig, Sigamond.**

Sinjin English form of *St. Jean,* Norman French place name. Sinjin Smith (beach volleyball champion).

Stoyan Bulgarian *stoya,* "stay, remain," originally given to a child whose older siblings had died in infancy. **Stoicho.**

Strom German "stream." Strom Thurmond (U.S. senator).

Sylvester Latin *silvester*, "woody." Sylvester Stallone (actor). **Silvester, Silvestre, Silvestro, Sylwester.**

Tate Old English *Tata*, uncertain meaning; or Old Norse *teitr*, "cheerful." Tate Donovan (actor). **Tait.**

Tau Tswana (Botswana) "lion."

Theron Greek "hunter." Theron Schlabach (historian).

Tizoc Nahuatl (Aztec) "sacred blood," name of seventh emperor of the Aztec empire. Used occasionally by modern Mexicans proud of their Native-American heritage. **Tezoc.**

Torquil Scots Gaelic *Torcaill*, from Norse *Torkild*, "Thor's cauldron." Considered an aristocratic name in Scotland.

Truman Middle English *treweman*, "trustworthy man." Truman Capote (author). **Trueman.**

Tyehimba Tiv (Nigeria) "we stand as a people."

Urban Latin *Urbanus*, "city dweller." **Orban.**

Valentine Latin *valens*, "strong, healthy, valiant." **Balint, Folant, Val, Valentin, Valentino, Velten, Walenty.**

Vance Old English *fenns*, "marshes." Vance Packard (author).

Varrick Origin unknown, possibly English "dwellings near a weir." Varrick Chittenden (folklorist). **Vareck, Warrick.**

Vartan Armenian "rose giver," from Persian *vart*, "rose." Vartan Gregorian (president of Brown University).

Velyo Old Bulgarian *velii*, "great." **Velcho, Velichko, Veliko, Velin, Velko.**

Vito Spanish and Italian form of Latin *vital*, "alive, lively"; also Italian form of **Victor.** Vito Russo (film critic and author). **Vite.**

Vladimir Slavonic *volod* [rule] + *meri* [great]. Vladimir Lenin (Russian revolutionary).

Vytautas Lithuanian, perhaps from *vytis* [knight] + *tautas* [nation]. Vytautas Landsbergis (President of Lithuania).

Wasant Marathi (western India) "spring."

Wayland Old English from *weg* [road] + *land*. Wayland the Smith (king of the elves in Old German folklore), Waylon Jennings (country musician). **Waylon.**

Willard Old English "bold resolve." Willard Scott (TV personality). **Will, Willy.**

Winthrop Old English place name, *Wina's thorp* or *Wigmund's thorp* from *thorp*, "farm or village." Winthrop Rockefeller (governor of Arkansas).

Xenos Greek "strange guest."

Yale Welsh *ial*, "fertile upland." Yale Kamisar (lawyer).

Zebadiah Hebrew "gift of God." **Zeb, Zebedee.**

Zikomo Ngoni (Malawi) "thank you."

Zoltan Hungarian *Szoltan*, form of Turkish *szultan*, "sultan, ruler." Zoltan Kodaly (composer).

Zubin Ancient Persian "the powerful sword." Zubin Mehta (conductor).

Most Popular Girls' Names

Abby (133) Form of **Abigail**. Abby Perkins (character on TV series *LA Law*). **Abbey, Abbi, Abbie.**

Abigail (86) Hebrew "father rejoices." Abigail Adams (spouse of President John Adams), Abigail Van Buren (columnist). **Abagail, Abbigail, Abby, Abigail, Abigayle, Gail.**

Adrian (447) Derivation same as boy's name **Adrian**. Adrian Balboa (spouse of title character in *Rocky* movies). **Adrien.**

Adriana (167) Italian and Spanish form of **Adrienne**. Adriana Bittel (novelist). **Adreana, Adrianna.**

Adrianne (462) Form of **Adrienne**. **Adriane, Adriann.**

Adrienne (196) French feminine form of **Adrian**, Latin "from the Adriatic." Adrienne Barbeau (actress), Adrienne Rich (poet). **Addy, Adrana, Adriana, Adrianne, Adriene.**

Alaina (290) Feminine form of **Alan**, perhaps Celtic "rock"; or a modern blend of **Alana** and **Elaine**. **Alayna.**

Alanna (189) Feminine form of **Alan**, perhaps Celtic "rock." Alana Cordy-Collins (anthropologist), Alannah Myles (singer). **Alana, Alannah, Lana, Lanna.**

Alex (438) Form of **Alexandra**. Alix
Pearlstein (sculptor). **Alix, Alyx.**

Alexa (148) Form of **Alexandra**. Alexa
Stirling Fraser (golfer).

Alexandra (48) Feminine form of Greek
Alexandros, "protector of mankind."
Alexandra Koltun (ballerina), Alexandra
Ripley (novelist). **Alejandra, Aleka,
Alessandra, Alex, Alexa, Alexandria,
Alexandrina, Alexandrine, Alexine, Lexie,
Lexine, Sandra, Sasha, Sondra, Zandra.**

Alexandria (81) Form of **Alexandra**.
Alexia.

Alexia (400) Short form of **Alexandria**.

Alexis (61) Greek "helper, defender." Alexis
Carrington Colby (character on TV series
Dynasty), Alexis Smith (actress). **Alexes,
Alexys.**

Ali (252) Form of **Alice** and **Allison**. Ali
McGraw, Ally Sheedy (actresses). **Alli, Allie,
Ally.**

Alia (365) Arabic "sublimity, loftiness."
Alea, Aleah, Aliya, Aliyah, Aliyyah.

Alice (328) Old German *adalhaidis*, "of noble
kind," from *athal* [noble] + *haidu* [kind,
rank], through Old French *adalis* or *alis*.
Alice Neel (artist), Alice Walker (author).
**Ali, Alicia, Alis, Alisa, Allison, Alyce, Alys,
Alyssa.**

Alicia (34) Latin form of **Alice.** Alicia Alonso (ballerina). **Aleasha, Alecia, Aleisha, Alesha, Aleshia, Alisha, Alishia, Alycia, Alyshia, Alyssa.**

Alina (424) Medieval short form of *Adelina,* a Latin form of Old German *adalheidis,* "of noble kind," from *athal* [noble] + *haidu* [kind, rank]. Alina Rodriguez (actress). **Aleena, Alena.**

Alisa (259) Russian form of **Alice.** Alisa Tager (art critic). **Alesa, Alysa.**

Allison (38) Old French *Alison,* form of **Alice.** Allison Hayes (actress), Alison Lurie (novelist). **Alicen, Alison, Allyson, Alyson, Alysson.**

Alyse (382) Modern blend of **Alice** and **Elise. Alease, Alise.**

Alysia (377) Modern blend of sounds of **Alicia** and **Elysia,** the latter from Greek *Elysion,* "abode of the blessed after death." **Alezha, Alisia.**

Alyssa (36) Form of **Alice** or **Alicia,** influenced by **Melissa** and the flower *alyssum.* Alyssa Katz (film critic). **Alissa, Allyssa.**

Amanda (4) Latin "worthy of love." Amanda Blake, Amanda Donohoe, Amanda Plummer (actresses). **Manda, Mandy.**

Amber (20) Arabic *anbar*, "amber," a pale yellow or green fossil resin used to make jewelry. Amber Roobenian (composer and organist). **Ambar, Ambur.**

Amberly (467) Old English *amore* [yellow-hammer bird] + *leah* [woodland glade], English place name. **Amberlee, Amberley.**

Amelia (180) German **Amalie,** from Old German *amal*, "work." Amelia Earhart (aviator). **Amalie, Amelina, Ameline, Amelita, Emily.**

Amy (40) Old French *amee*, "beloved." Amy Irving, Amy Madigan (actresses), Amy Tan (novelist). **Aime, Aimee, Ame, Ami, Amie, Amye.**

Anastasia (287) Feminine form of Greek *anastasis*, "resurrection." Anastasia Toufexis (journalist), Nastassja Kinski (actress). **Anstice, Nastasia, Nastassja, Natya, Stacy.**

Andrea (55) Feminine form of **Andrew,** Greek "manly." Andrea Dworkin (feminist), Andrea Martin (comedienne). **Andi, Andree, Andria.**

Angel (166) Form of **Angela.** Angel Martino (Olympic swimmer). **Aingeal, Angell.**

Angela (60) Greek *angelos*, "angel" or "messenger." Angela Carter (author), Angela Lansbury (actress). **Andela, Angel, Angelia. Angelina, Angeline, Angelique, Angie, Anjela.**

Angelia (302) Modern form of **Angela.**
Angelea, Angeleah.

Angelica (164) Feminine form of Latin
angelicus, "angelic." Anjelica Huston
(actress). **Anjelica.**

Angelina (260) Spanish and Italian form of
Angela. Angelina Grimke (abolitionist).

Anita (464) Spanish form of **Ann.** Anita
Baker (singer). **Aneta.**

Anna (51) Latin and Greek form of Hebrew
hannah, "grace" or "God has favored me."
Anna Karenina (title character in Tolstoi
novel), Anna Quindlen (columnist), Anna
Pavlova (ballerina). **Ana, Anne.**

Anne (113) French and English form of
Anna. Ann Landers (columnist), Anne
Murray (singer), Ann Richards (governor of
Texas). **Ann.**

Annelise (442) German blend of **Anne** and
Elise. Anneliese Wagner (poet). **Annalise,
Anneliese.**

Annie (313) Form of **Ann.** Annie Dillard
(author), Annie Potts (actress). **Anny.**

Ansley (479) Old English *Anesteleye,*
probably from *ansetl* [hermitage] + *leah*
[glade]. **Annesley, Annsley.**

Antoinette (315) Feminine form of
Antoine. Antoinette Perry (Broadway
actress, director, and producer). **Antwanette,
Antwonette, Toni.**

April (79) Latin *aprilis*, the fourth month in
the calendar, probably from *apru*, Etruscan
form of Aphrodite, the Greek goddess of love.
April Ulring Larson (Lutheran bishop).
Apryl, Avril.

Ariana (221) Latin form of Greek **Ariadne,**
"very holy one"; in Greek mythology, the
princess from Crete who helped Theseus
escape from the Minotaur. Arianna Randolph
Wormeley (dramatist). **Arianna.**

Ariel (97) Hebrew "lion of God." A male
name in the Bible and modern Israel, but
used primarily for females in the U.S. Ariel
Durant (historian), Ariel (heroine of film *The
Little Mermaid*). **Airial, Arial, Eriel.**

Arielle (185) French feminine form of **Ariel.**
Ariele.

Ashley (2) Old English *aescleah,* "meadow
with ash trees." Most popular girls' name in
U.S. between 1984 and 1989. Ashley Putnam
(operatic soprano). **Ashlea, Ashlee, Ashleigh,
Ashli, Ashlie, Ashly.**

Ashlyn (361) Modern blend of **Ashley** and
Lynn; or American form of **Ashling,** a
modern Irish name from Gaelic *aisling,*
"dream" or "vision." **Ashlin, Ashlynn.**

Ashton (249) English place name, "ash tree farm." Ashton Main (character in novel *North and South*). **Ashtan, Ashten, Ashtin, Ashtun, Ashtyn.**

Asia (272) Name of the continent, from a Greek word meaning "east"; also occasionally a form of **Iesha. Asya, Aysia.**

Aubrey (171) French form of Old German *Albirich*, from *alfi* [elf] + *ric* [ruler]. Aubrey Beardsley (male English artist). **Aubree, Aubri, Aubrie, Aubry.**

Audrey (157) Old English *Aethelthryth*, "noble strength." Audrey Hepburn (actress). **Audie, Audra, Audre, Audrie, Audry, Audrye.**

Audrianna (441) Modern creation blending **Audrey** and **Adriana. Audriana, Audrionna.**

Autumn (150) Latin *autumnus*, the season. **Autum.**

Ayana (455) Origin unclear, perhaps an African-American form of Somali *Ayan*, "bright"; or Yoruba (Nigeria) *Ayo*, "joy." **Ayanna, Ayonna, Iyana.**

Bailey (168) Old French *bailif*, "manager, local official"; or *baile*, "wall of the outer court of a castle." Bailey Quarters (character in TV series *WKRP in Cincinnati*), Bailey White (teacher and writer). **Bailee, Baileigh, Baylee, Bayleigh, Baylie.**

Barbara (192) Greek *barbaros,* "strange,
foreign." Barbara Bush (spouse of President
Bush), Barbara Mikulski (U.S. senator),
Barbra Streisand (singer, actress, director).
**Babette, Babs, Barb, Barbel, Barbie, Barbra,
Barbro, Bobbi, Borbala, Varvara.**

Beatriz (468) Spanish form of **Beatrice,**
Latin *beatrix,* "bringer of joy." Beatrice
Arthur (actress), Beatrix (Queen of the
Netherlands). **Bea, Beatrice, Beatris, Beatrix.**

Beth (327) Form of **Elizabeth** or **Bethany;**
also Hebrew *Bethia,* "daughter of the Lord."
Beth Henley (playwright), Beth Osborne
Daponte (demographer). **Bet.**

Bethany (95) Biblical place name, Aramaic
"house of poverty." Bethany Pray (poet).
Beth, Bethanie, Betheny.

Betty (458) Form of **Elizabeth.** Especially
popular in the 1940s due to fame of
actresses Bette Davis, Betty Grable, and
Betty Hutton. Betty Friedan (author), Bette
Midler (singer and actress). **Bet, Bette,
Bettie.**

Beverly (450) Old English *beferlic,* "beaver
stream." Beverly D'Angelo (actress), Beverly
Sills (operatic soprano). **Bev, Beverlee,
Beverley, Buffy.**

Bianca (115) Italian "white." Bianca Jagger
(celebrity). **Beanka, Beonca, Bionca, Bionka.**

Blair (374) Celtic "flat land," Scottish place name. Blair Brown (actress). **Blaire, Blayre.**

Bobbi (331) Feminine form of **Robert;** also variation of **Barbara.** Bobbie Gentry (singer), Bobbie Ann Mason (writer). **Bobbie, Bobby.**

Bonnie (317) Scottish *bonny,* "a pretty girl," from Old French *bonne,* "good." Bonnie Bedelia (actress), Bonnie Blair (speed skater), Bonnie Strickland (psychologist). **Bonny.**

Brandi (54) Dutch *brandewijn,* "burnt wine," or a feminine form of **Brandon.** Brandy Johnson (gymnast). **Brandee, Brandie, Brandy.**

Breanna (90) Modern blend of **Bree** (Irish short form of **Bridget**) and **Anna,** or variation of **Brianna. Breana, Breeanna, Breonna, Brieanna.**

Breanne (255) Blend of **Bree** and **Anne,** or variation of **Brianne. Breann, Breeanne, Brieanne.**

Brenda (232) Feminine form of Old Norse *Brandr,* "sword"; also feminine form of **Brendan.** Brenda Putnam (sculptor), Brenda Vaccaro (actress).

Brenna (390) Probably a feminine form of **Brennan. Brennah.**

Brianna (45) Feminine form of **Brian**.
Breanna, Briana, Bryana, Bryanna.

Brianne (267) Modern feminine form of
Brian. Breanne, Briann, Bryanne.

Bridget (121) Celtic *Brigenti*, "the high
goddess." Brigitte Bardot, Bridget Fonda
(actresses). **Biddy, Birgit, Bree, Bride,
Bridgett, Bridgette, Bridgie, Brigette, Brigid,
Brigida, Brigitte, Brita.**

Brittany (1) From French *Bretagne*, a
region of France settled by Celtic refugees
from Britain. **Britani, Britany, Britiny,
Britney, Britni, Britny, Brittaney, Brittani,
Brittanie, Britteny, Brittiny, Brittnee,
Brittney, Brittni, Brittnie, Brittny.**

Brooke (65) Old English, "brook, stream."
Brooke Adams, Brooke Shields (actresses).
Brook.

Brynn (492) Welsh *bryn*, "hill." Primarily a
male name in Wales, a female name in the
U.S. **Brinn, Bryn, Brynne.**

Caitlin (9) Irish Gaelic form of *Cateline*, Old
French form of **Katherine. Caitlin** is really
the Gaelic spelling of **Kathleen,** but in the
U.S. it is pronounced as if a combination of
Kate and **Lynn.** Caitlin Brune (experimental
psychologist), Caitlin Thomas (writer).
**Caitlan, Caitlyn, Caitlynn, Catelyn, Kaitlin,
Kaitlyn, Kaitlynn, Katelin, Katelyn,
Katelynn, Kaytlin.**

Callie (173) Short form of four different nineteenth-century names: **Calista,** from Greek *Kallistos,* "most beautiful"; **Calliope,** Greek *Kalliope,* "beautiful voice," name of one of the Muses; **Caledonia,** Latin name for Scotland; and **Calvina,** feminine form of **Calvin.** Callie Khouri (screenwriter). **Calli, Cally, Kalli, Kallie, Kally.**

Cameron (445) Scottish Gaelic, either *camshron,* "crooked nose," or from a place name, "crooked hill." **Cameren, Cameronne, Kamerin, Kamryn.**

Camille (213) French form of **Camilla,** possibly Etruscan through Latin *Camillus,* "acolyte." Camille (title character of 1936 movie starring Greta Garbo). **Kami.**

Candace (68) A title of Ethiopian queens, uncertain meaning. Candice Bergen (actress). **Candice, Candis, Candy, Kandace, Kandice, Kandis, Kandyce.**

Candy (451) Form of **Candace** or **Candida.** Candy Dulfer (saxophonist). **Candi, Candie, Kandi, Kandie, Kandy.**

Carissa (137) Latin form of Greek *charis,* "grace," or Italian "little dear one." **Caresse, Carisa, Caryssa, Charissa, Karissa.**

Carly (89) A feminine form of **Carl,** Old German "a man or farmer"; also a form of **Carol.** Carly Simon (singer). **Carlee, Carleigh, Carley, Carli, Carlie, Karli, Karlie, Karly.**

Carmen (261) Spanish form of **Carmel,**
Hebrew "the garden." Carmen (title character
in Bizet opera), Carmen Miranda (actress).
Carman, Carmina, Karmen, Karmyn.

Carol (307) A shortened form of **Caroline,**
later associated with French "song." Carol
Burnett (comedienne); Carol Channing, Carol
Kane, Carole Lombard (actresses). **Carly,
Carole, Carroll, Caryl, Karol.**

Carolina (351) Latin and Spanish form of
Caroline. Carolina Herrera (fashion
designer). **Karolina.**

Caroline (122) Italian feminine form of
Charles. Caroline (Princess of Monaco),
Caroline Kennedy (lawyer and daughter of
President Kennedy). **Carlin, Caro, Carol,
Caroliana, Carolina, Carolyn, Carrie, Kara,
Karla, Karoline.**

Carolyn (152) Form of **Caroline.** Carolyn
Sapp (Miss America for 1992), Carolyn
Waldo (swimmer).

Carrie (118) Form of **Caroline.** Carrie Fisher
(actress), Carrie Chapman Catt (suffragist),
Carrie Mae Weems (photographer). **Carey,
Cari, Carie, Carri, Carry, Karie, Karri, Karrie.**

Casey (49) From Gaelic *Cathasach,*
"watchful." **Caci, Casie, Cayce, Kacee, Kacey,
Kaci, Kacie, Kacy, Kasey.**

Cassandra (46) Greek, uncertain meaning.
Cassandra was the daughter of Priam and
Hecuba, the king and queen of ancient Troy,
and is remembered for her gift of prophecy.
Cassandra Wilson (jazz singer). **Casandra,
Cass, Cassaundra, Cassie, Cassondra,
Kasandra, Kassandra, Sandra, Sandy.**

Cassidy (266) Irish Gaelic *O Caiside*,
surname of unknown meaning. **Cassady,
Cassidee, Cassie, Kassidi, Kassidy.**

Cassie (143) Form of **Cassandra** and
Cassidy.

Catherine (see **Katherine**).

Cecilia (335) Feminine form of **Cecil**, Latin
caecus, "blind." Cecilia Holland (novelist),
Cecilia Ridgeway (sociologist). **Cecelia, Cecile,
Cecily, Celia, Celie, Cicely, Ciel, Cissie, Sheila.**

Cecily (394) English form of **Cecilia**. Cicely
Tyson (actress). **Cecelie, Cicely.**

Celeste (406) French form of **Celestine** from
Latin *caelestis*, "heavenly." Celeste Holm
(actress), Celeste Susnis (cross-country
runner). **Celesta, Celestina, Celestine,
Celestyn.**

Chanel (203) French surname from *chenal*,
"canal," later trade name of famous perfume.
**Chanell, Chanelle, Channell, Chenelle,
Shanel, Shanell, Shanelle.**

Chantal (383) Old French *cantal,* "stone, stony place," from Jeanne de Chantal, a seventeenth-century French saint. Chantal (Hollywood entertainment reporter). **Chantale, Chantalle, Chantel, Shantal.**

Chantel (142) American variation of **Chantal.** The Chantels (1950s female rock group). **Chantell, Chantelle, Shantel, Shantelle, Shontel, Shontell.**

Charity (380) Middle English *charite,* from Latin *caritas,* "spiritual love." Charity (character in Broadway musical and movie *Sweet Charity*). **Charitie.**

Charlee (453) Form of **Charles** or **Charlene. Charli, Charlie.**

Charlene (296) Feminine form of **Charles.** Charlene Tilton (actress). **Char, Charleen, Charlie, Sharlene.**

Charlotte (300) French feminine form of **Charles.** Charlotte Bronte (novelist), Charlotte Rampling (actress). **Carlotta, Lotta, Lottie.**

Charmaine (488) Origin unclear, but probably invented in England around 1920 as a "French-sounding" form of **Charmian,** a Shakespearean name from Greek *charma,* "joy." Charmaine Neville (singer). **Charmain, Charmayne, Sharmaine, Sharmane.**

Chasity (295) Modern American variation of
Chastity, Latin *castitas,* "sexual purity,"
perhaps arising from misunderstanding name
of Chastity Bono (daughter of entertainers
Sonny and Cher). **Chasaty, Chasiti, Chasitie,
Chassity, Chastity.**

Chelsea (19) English place name, "landing
place for chalk," and part of a borough of
Greater London on the north bank of the
River Thames. Current popularity may have
been influenced by character played by Jane
Fonda in movie *On Golden Pond.* Chelsea
Quinn Yarbro (author). **Chelcie, Chelsee,
Chelsey, Chelsi, Chelsie.**

Cherelle (395) Modern creation blending
Cheryl or **Sharon** with ending of **Michelle,
Janelle,** and similar base names. Cherrell
Guilfoyle (theater historian). **Cherrell,
Cherrelle, Sharelle, Sherrell, Sherrelle.**

Cherie (321) French *chere,* "cherished,
beloved." **Chel, Cher, Chere, Cheree, Cheri,
Cheryl, Sheree, Sherie, Sheryl.**

Cherise (342) Form of **Charisse,** itself a
French form of Greek *charis,* "grace." Made
famous by dancer and actress Cyd Charisse.
**Charice, Charise, Charisse, Cherese, Cherice,
Shareese, Sharice, Sherise.**

Cheryl (301) Uncertain origin, probably
created about 1900 by combining **Cherie** or
Cherry with **Beryl.** Cheryl Crawford
(theatrical producer), Cheryl Ladd (actress).
Charyl, Sherrill, Sheryl.

Cheyenne (233) Native American nation, unknown meaning. Cheyenne Brando (daughter of Marlon Brando). **Cheyanne, Sheyenne, Shianne, Shyann, Shyanne.**

Chloe (216) Greek *kloe*, "green, young plant." **Clo, Cloe.**

Christian (211) Derivation same as boy's name **Christian.**

Christina (22) Feminine form of **Christian.** Cristina Garcia (novelist), Christina Paxson (economist). **Chris, Christine, Chrystina, Cristina, Kirsten, Kirstie, Krista, Kristen, Kristi, Kristina, Krystina, Krystyna, Tina.**

Christine (59) French feminine form of **Christian.** Christine Kaufmann, Christine Lahti (actresses). **Christene, Cristine, Kristi, Kristine, Krystine.**

Ciara (207) In the U.S., usually taken from trade name of a perfume and pronounced either as "see-ARE-uh" or **Sierra;** in Ireland, it is pronounced as "Keera." **Ciarra, Cieara, Kira, Siara.**

Cindy (339) Form of **Cynthia, Lucinda,** or (very rarely) **Cinderella.** Cindy Crawford (model), Cyndi Lauper (singer). **Cyndi.**

Claire (156) French form of **Clara,** itself the feminine form of Latin *clarus*, "bright, clear." Claire Bloom (actress), Clare Booth Luce (editor, playwright, member of Congress). **Clair, Clare, Clarissa, Klaire.**

Clarissa (323) Form of **Claire** or **Clara**. Full
first name of Clara Barton (founder of
American Red Cross). **Clairissa, Klarissa.**

Claudia (358) Feminine form of **Claudius**,
Latin "lame." Claudia Cardinale (actress).
Claudette, Claudine, Gladys.

Codi (357) Feminine form of **Cody. Codee,
Codie, Cody, Kodee, Kodi, Kodie, Kody.**

Colleen (174) Irish Gaelic *cailin,* "girl." Not
used as a name in Ireland, but popular with
Americans and Australians of Irish ancestry.
Colleen Dewhurst (actress), Colleen
McCullough (author). **Colene, Collene.**

Constance (461) Latin *constantia,*
"constancy." Constance Bennett (actress),
Constance Baker Motley (U.S. federal judge).
Connie, Constancia, Constancy, Constanza.

Cori (182) Short form of **Cora, Corinne,** or
Cornelia; or feminine form of **Corey.** Corrie
ten Boom (Dutch Christian who saved Jews
from the Nazis). **Corey, Corie, Corri, Corrie,
Cory, Kori, Korri, Kory.**

Corinne (277) French variation of **Cora;**
probably Greek *kore,* "girl." Corinne Cobson
(fashion designer). **Corine, Corrinne, Corynn,
Korinn, Korynne.**

Courtney (15) Middle English *de Curtenay,*
from *Courtney,* a French place name.
Courteney Cox (actress). **Cortney, Cortni,
Courteney, Courtnie, Kortney, Kourtney.**

Crystal (35) Greek *krystalos*, "rock crystal, clear ice." Krystle Carrington (character on TV series *Dynasty*), Crystal Gayle (singer). **Christal, Chrystal, Cristal, Kristal, Krystal, Krystle.**

Cynthia (131) A title of the Greek moon goddess, Artemis, from Mt. Cynthus, where she was worshipped. Cynthia Gregory (ballerina), Cynthia Phelps (violinist). **Cinda, Cindy, Cinthia, Cintia.**

Daisy (437) Old English *daeges-eage*, "the day's eye," because the flower looks like the sun. Daisy Fuentes (host on MTV). **Daisie, Daysi.**

Dakota (449) Name of Native American nation. **Dakotah.**

Dana (108) Perhaps Old English "from Denmark"; also a variation of **Daniele.** Dana Delany (actress). **Daina, Dayna.**

Danica (359) Form of **Danika,** a Slavic name meaning "morning star." Danica McKellar (actress on TV series *The Wonder Years*). **Danika.**

Daniela (348) Spanish form of **Danielle.** Daniela O'Neill (psychologist).

Danielle (26) French feminine form of **Daniel,** Hebrew "God is my judge." Danielle Steel (novelist). **Danelle, Dani, Daniela, Daniele, Danita, Dannielle, Danya, Danyel, Danyelle.**

Darcy (454) French *d'Arcy*, "from Arcy,"
French place name; or form of Irish Gaelic
O Dorchaidhe, "dark man's descendant."
Darci Kistler (ballerina). **Darci, Darcie.**

Dawn (282) Old English *dagian*, "daybreak."
Dawn Riley (crew member in America's Cup
yacht race), Dawn Upshaw (opera singer).

Deanna (149) Feminine form of **Dean,** or
variation of **Diana.** Deanna Durbin (actress).

Deborah (181) Hebrew "bee." Deborah
Norville (TV reporter), Debra Winger
(actress). **Deb, Debbie, Debora, Debra,
Debrah, Devorah.**

Deidra (459) American form of **Deirdre,**
name of a tragic heroine in ancient Irish
legend, perhaps meaning "chatterer."
Deedra, Dedra, Diedra.

Dena (376) Variation of **Dinah,** Hebrew
"vindicated"; short form of **Bernardina,**
feminine of **Bernard;** or feminine form of
Dean. Dena Shottenkirk (art critic). **Deana,
Deena, Dina.**

Denise (210) French feminine form of
Dennis. Denise Scott Brown (architect).
Denice, Denisse, Denni, Denyse.

Denisha (352) African-American creation,
blending beginning of **Denise** or **Danielle** with
-isha. **Danesha, Danisha, Deneisha, Denesha.**

Desiree (101) French "desired one." Desiree Clary (French woman who became queen of Sweden). **Desarae, Deserae, Desirae, Desirea, Dezirae.**

Destiny (144) Middle English *destinee,* "fortune, fate," from Latin *destinata,* "established." **Destany, Destinee, Destiney, Destyni.**

Devon (119) English county name, "land of the Dumnonii (a Celtic tribe)." **Devan, Deven, Devin, Devyn** (and see **Devin** in section on popular boys' names).

Diamond (444) Old French *diamant,* "diamond." **Dymond.**

Diana (130) Roman goddess of the moon, probably from Greek *deus,* "god, divine," through Latin *dius.* Diana, Princess of Wales; Diana Ross (singer and actress). **Deanna, Di, Diane, Dianna, Dyan.**

Diane (322) French form of **Diana.** Diane Feinstein (politician), Dyan Cannon, Diane Keaton (actresses); Diane Schur (jazz singer). **Diahann, Dian, Dianne, Dyan, Dyanne.**

Dominique (165) French feminine form of **Dominic.** Dominique Dawes (Olympic gymnast). **Domanique, Domenique, Domineek, Domineke.**

Donna (304) Italian, from Latin *domina,*
"lady," though often used as a feminine form
of **Donald.** Donna Summer (singer). **Dona,
Donella, Donnie.**

Dorothy (353) Latin reversed form of Greek
theodora, "gift of god." Dorothy (heroine in
The Wizard of Oz), Dorothy Hamill (figure
skater), Dorothy Parker (author). **Doll, Dolly,
Doreen, Dorina, Doro, Dorota, Dorothea, Dot,
Dottie.**

Ebony (163) Middle English *hebeny* from
Latin *ebenus,* "black." Used as a first name
since about 1970. **Ebeny, Ebonee, Eboni,
Ebonie, Ebyni.**

Eileen (373) Irish *Eibhlin,* originally a form
of **Evelyn,** though later also used as Irish
form of **Helen.** Eileen Goudge (novelist),
Aileen Quinn (actress). **Aileen, Ailene,
Ailleen, Ilene.**

Elaine (407) Form of *Helaine,* an Old French
form of **Helen.** Elaine May (comedienne and
film director). **Elayne.**

Elena (393) Spanish form of **Helen.** Elena
Castedo (novelist).

Elisa (408) Form of **Elizabeth.** Elisa D'Arrigo
(sculptor). **Eliza.**

Elise (187) French form of **Elizabeth.** Elyse
Keaton (character on TV series *Family Ties*).
Elyse.

Elisha (378) A blend of **Elise** and **Alicia** (though as a boy's name it would be Hebrew "God is salvation"). **Eleasha, Eleisha, Elesha, Elicia, Ellisha.**

Elissa (474) Form of **Elizabeth,** or the Phoenician name of Dido, legendary queen who founded ancient Carthage. Elissa Benedek (psychiatrist), Elissa Landi (actress). **Elyssa.**

Eliza (475) Short form of **Elizabeth** used since sixteenth century. Eliza Doolittle (central character in musical *My Fair Lady*), Eliza Haywood (dramatist).

Elizabeth (18) Hebrew *Elisheba,* "my God is my oath." Elizabeth Barret Browning (poet), Elizabeth Taylor (actress). **Babette, Bessie, Bet, Beth, Betsy, Betty, Elisa, Elisabeth, Elisabetta, Elise, Elissa, Eliza, Elsa, Elspeth, Elzbieta, Erzsebet, Isabel, Isabella, Libby, Lisa, Lisbeth, Lissette, Liz, Liza, Lizabeth, Lizzie, Yelizaveta.**

Ellen (208) English variation of **Helen.** Ellen Barkin, Ellen Burstyn (actresses); Ellen Goodman (columnist). **Ellie, Ellyn.**

Emily (13) Medieval form of *Aemilius,* Roman clan name of uncertain meaning, but confused with **Amelia** since eighteenth century. Emily Bronte (novelist), Emily Dickinson (poet). **Em, Emely, Emilee, Emilie, Emmi.** (See **Amelia**).

Emma (138) Old German form of *ermin*, "whole, universal." Emma Thompson (actress), Emma Stebbins (sculptor). **Emmy.**

Erica (31) Feminine form of **Eric,** possibly Old German "ever-ruler." Erica Jong (author), Erica Kane (character on TV series *All My Children*). **Arica, Ericka, Erika, Rikki.**

Erin (44) Gaelic *Eireann*, perhaps "western island," another name for Ireland. Erin Gray (actress). **Aryn, Erina, Erinn, Eryn.**

Esther (392) Possibly from Persian *satarah*, "star, the planet Venus." Esther Rolle (actress). **Essie, Ester, Hester.**

Eva (399) Latin form of Hebrew *hawwah*, "life." Eva Chun (fashion designer), Eva Marie Saint (actress). **Eve, Evie.**

Evelyn (347) Old German *Avelina*, feminine form of *Avi*, ancient Germanic name of unknown meaning. Evelyn Ashford (sprinter), Evelyn Wood (promoter of speed reading). **Aveline, Eveleen, Eveline.**

Faith (271) Latin *fides*, "belief in God" or "trust," through Old French *feid*. Faith Baldwin (novelist), Faith Prince (actress). **Fae, Fay, Faye, Fayth, Faythe.**

Felicia (98) Feminine form of **Felix,** Latin "happy." Felicia Farr, Phylicia Rashad (actresses). **Falisha, Felecia, Felica, Felice, Felicity, Felisha, Phylicia.**

Frances (340) Feminine form of **Francis,**
Latin "a Frank." Frances Sternhagen
(actress). **Fanny, Fran, Francesca, Francine,
Francisca, Francoise, Frannie, Franziska.**

Francesca (480) Italian form of **Frances.**
Francesca Annis (actress).

Gabriela (193) Spanish form of **Gabrielle.**
Gabriela Sabatini (tennis player). **Gabriella.**

Gabrielle (102) Feminine form of **Gabriel,**
Hebrew "man of God." Gabrielle "Coco"
Chanel (clothing and perfume designer).
Gabriela, Gaby.

Genevieve (417) Probably a French form of
Genovefa, Old German from *genos* [race of
people] + *wefa* [woman]. Genevieve Bujold
(actress). **Gen, Geneva, Geni, Genoveffa,
Genoveva, Ginevra, Javotte, Jenny.**

Gianna (484) Italian form of **Jane.**

Gina (111) Form of **Eugenia** (feminine form
of **Eugene**), **Regina,** or **Luigina.** Geena Davis,
Gina Lollobrigida (actresses). **Geena, Gena.**

Gloria (338) Latin "glory." Gloria Steinem
(writer and publisher). **Gloriana, Glory.**

Grace (145) Latin *gratia,* "grace." Grace
Jones (actress and model), Grace Kelly
(actress and Princess of Monaco). **Gracia,
Gracie, Graciela, Gratia, Grayce, Grazia.**

Gretchen (481) German variation of
Margaret. Gretchen Carlson (former Miss
America), Gretchen Vanzandt Merrill
(Olympic skater). **Greta, Gretel.**

Haley (58) Form of **Hayley,** Old English
Hayley, "hay clearing"; or, rarely, a form of
Mahala, an Old Testament Hebrew name
possibly meaning "harp." Hayley Mills
(actress). **Hailee, Hailey, Haleigh, Haylee,
Hayley.**

Hallie (471) American form of **Harriet** from
the nineteenth century (compare **Hal** from
Harry or **Harold**). Hallie Erminie Rives
(novelist). **Halley.**

Hannah (37) Hebrew "the Lord has favored
me." Hannah Arendt (historian), Hannah
Storm (TV sportscaster). **Hana, Hanna,
Hannie.**

Heather (25) Middle English *hathir,*
"heather." Heather Locklear (actress),
Heather Swanson (historian). **Heath.**

Heidi (186) Form of **Adelaide,** Old German
adelhaid, "noble rank." Heidi (title character
in famous children's story by Johanna
Spyri). **Heide, Heidy.**

Helen (356) Greek *Helene,* "bright, shining
one." Helen Keller (author and educator),
Helen Reddy (singer). **Eileen, Elaine,**

Eleanor, Elena, Ellen, Helena, Helene, Ileana,
Ilona, Lena, Nell, Nellie, Yelena.

Hillary (114) Latin *hilaris*, "cheerful,
pleasant." Hillary Clinton (lawyer and spouse
of President Clinton). **Hilary, Hillari.**

Holly (75) Old English *holegn*, "holly." Holly
Hunter (actress), Holly Near (singer and
songwriter). **Hollee, Holley, Holli, Hollie.**

Hope (222) Old English *hopa*, "hope." Hope
Lange (actress).

Iesha (204) Arabic *A'isha*, "alive and well";
name of the favorite wife of the prophet
Mohammed. **Aisha, Asha, Ashia, Asia,
Ayesha, Ayisha, Ieasha, Iisha.**

India (366) Name of the Asian country, from
Sanskrit *sindhuh*, "river." India Edwards
(journalist and politician). **Indya.**

Isabel (413) Spanish and Portuguese form of
Elizabeth. Isabelle Adjani, Isabella Rossellini
(actresses). **Bell, Isa, Isabella, Isabelle,
Isobel, Izzy, Ysabel.**

Jackie (402) Form of **Jacqueline.** Jackie
Joyner-Kersee (Olympic athlete).

Jaclyn (123) Form of **Jacqueline.** Jaclyn
Smith (actress). **Jacalyn, Jackeline, Jacklyn,
Jacklynn, Jaclynn.**

Jacqueline (63) Feminine form of **Jacques**, itself the French form of **James** or **Jacob**. Jacqueline Kennedy Onassis (editor and widow of President Kennedy). **Jackie, Jaclyn, Jacquelin, Jacqueline, Jacquelyn, Jacquelynn, Jaqueline.**

Jacy (485) Origin unknown, though possibly a feminine form of **Jace** or **Jason**, or a respelling of the initials **J.C. Jaci, Jacie, Jasie, Jaycee, Jaycie.**

Jade (202) Italian *giada*, "jade," from Spanish *ijada*, "colic," because jade (the green gemstone) was believed to help cure colic. Jade Li (entomologist). **Jayde.**

Jaleesa (212) African-American creation, *Ja-* + **Lisa**. Jaleesa Vinson (character on TV series *A Different World*). **Gelisa, Jaleisa, Jalesa, Jalisa, Jelisa, Jillisa.**

Jamie (41) Feminine form of **James**, Hebrew "the supplanter." Jamie Lee Curtis, Jami Gertz (actresses). **Jaime, Jaimee, Jaimie, Jamee, Jamey, Jami, Jayme, Jaymie.**

Jamila (410) Arabic and Swahili "beautiful." **Jameelah, Jamilah.**

Jana (318) Slavic and Scandinavian form of **Jane**. Jana Napoli (artist). **Janna.**

Janae (242) Modern American respelling of French pronunciation of **Janet. Janay, Janaye.**

Jane (349) Feminine form of **John.** Jane
Fonda, Jane Alexander, Jane Seymour
(actresses); Jane Austen (novelist). **Gianna,
Giovanna, Jan, Jana, Janae, Janelle, Janet,
Janette, Janice, Janie, Jayne, Jean, Jeanne,
Jenny, Joan, Joanna, Johanna, Jonna,
Juana, Sheena, Siobhan.**

Janelle (178) Modern American form of
Jane. Janel Curry-Roper (geographer).
Janel, Janell.

Janessa (404) Modern blend of **Janet** or
Janice and **Vanessa.**

Janet (311) Feminine form of **John;**
especially popular in Scotland. Janet Evans
(Olympic swimmer), Janet Guthrie (race car
driver), Janet Lynn (figure skater). **Janette.**

Janice (440) Feminine form of **John,**
created in 1899 by American novelist Paul
Leicester Ford for heroine of his book *Janice
Meredith.* Janis Joplin (singer), Janice
Merrill (track athlete). **Janis, Sinead.**

Janie (497) Form of **Jane.** Janie Eickhoff
(cyclist). **Janey.**

Jasmine (30) Persian *yasemin,* a flower
name. Jasmine Guy (actress). **Jasmin,
Jasmyn, Jazmin, Jazmine, Jazmyn, Jazz,
Jessamine, Yasmin.**

Jeanette (360) French feminine form of **John.** Jeanette Kastenberg (fashion designer), Jeannette Rankin (member of Congress). **Jeannette, Jennette.**

Jenna (88) Form of **Jenny** or **Jennifer.** Jenna Wade (character on TV series *Dallas*). **Genna, Jennah.**

Jennifer (14) Cornish form of Welsh *Gwenhwyfar*, from *gwen* [white] + *hwyfar* [yielding, smooth]. Jennifer Capriati (tennis player), Jennifer Jason Leigh (actress). **Gennifer, Jen, Jenifer, Jenna, Jennie, Jenny.**

Jenny (188) Form of **Jennifer, Genevieve,** and **Jane.** Jenny Jones (comedienne), Jennie Livingston (documentary filmmaker). **Jenna, Jenni, Jennie.**

Jerrica (254) Recent creation forming a feminine name from **Jerry** or **Jeremy** on the model of **Jessica** or **Erica. Gerrica, Jarica, Jarrica, Jerica, Jerika.**

Jessica (3) Feminine form of **Jesse,** Hebrew "God exists." Jessica Lange, Jessica Tandy (actresses). **Jess, Jessalyn, Jesse, Jessie.**

Jessie (158) Originally a Scottish form of **Janet,** now a form of **Jessica.** Jessie Stagg (sculptor), Jessye Norman (operatic soprano). **Jesse, Jessi, Jessy, Jessye.**

Jill (310) Form of **Jillian.** Jill Eikenberry (actress), Jill Johnston (author). **Jilliana, Jillie, Jilly.**

Jillian (126) Middle English *Gillian*, a
variation of **Juliana. Gillian, Jill.**

Joanna (184) Form of **Johanna.** Joanna
Cassidy (actress), Joanna Russ (novelist).
Jo, Joanne, Jodi.

Joanne (416) French feminine form of
Joanna. Joann Levy (historian), Joanne
Woodward (actress). **Jo, Jo Ann, Joann.**

Jocelyn (153) Norman French form of Old
German *gautelen*, probably "of the Goths."
**Joscelin, Joscelyn, Joselyn, Joslyn,
Josselyn, Yoselyn.**

Jodi (280) Short form of **Joanna** or **Judith.**
Jodi Bilinkoff (historian), Jodie Foster
(actress and director). **Jodee, Jodie, Jody.**

Johanna (388) Latin feminine form of
John. Johanna Schmitt (botanist). **Joanna.**

Jordan (56) Derivation same as boy's name
Jordan. Jordin, Jordyn, Jourdan.

Josie (418) Variation of **Josephine,** a
feminine form of **Joseph.** Josie Cruz Natori
(clothing designer). **Josey.**

Joy (312) Old French *joie,* "joy." Joie Lee
(actress). **Joi, Joie, Joya.**

Julia (91) Feminine form of **Julian,** a Latin
family name. Julia Child (food expert), Julia
Howe (suffragist), Julia Roberts (actress).
Juliana, Julie.

Juliana (375) Medieval variation of **Julia,**
Julianna Walworth (equestrian). **Gillian,
Julianna, Julianne.**

Julianne (332) French form of **Juliana.**
Julianne Baird (singer), Julianne Phillips
(actress), Julianne Turko (geologist).

Julie (92) French form of **Julia.** Julie
Andrews, Julie Harris (actresses). **Julee.**

Justina (472) Latin form of **Justine.**
Justina Hamilton Hill (bacteriologist).

Justine (227) French feminine form of
Justin, Latin "the just." Justine Bateman
(actress). **Justina.**

Kady (354) Form of **Cady,** Scottish Gaelic
Cadda, "battle"; or modern creation using
Kay + **Dee.** Kady MacDonald Denton
(illustrator). **Cadi, Cadie, Cady, Kadee,
Kady, Kaydee, Kaydie.**

Kali (325) Sanskrit "dark goddess."

Kami (367) Short form of **Camille.** Kami
Cotler (actress, Elizabeth on TV series *The
Waltons*). **Cami, Cammi, Cammie, Cammy,
Kamee, Kammi, Kammie, Kammy.**

Kamisha (496) African-American creation
blending **Kami** and *-isha.* **Camiesha,
Camisha, Kameisha, Kamesha, Kamicia.**

Kanisha (155) African-American creation
blending *Ka-* + *-n-* + *-isha*, or a feminine
form of **Kenneth. Kaneesha, Kaneisha,
Kanesha, Keneisha, Kenesha, Kenicia,
Kenisha.**

Kara (71) Latin *cara*, feminine of *carus*,
"dear"; or form of **Kathryn** or **Caroline.**
Kara Meyers (fashion model). **Cara.**

Karen (124) Danish form of **Katherine.**
Karen Allen, Karen Valentine (actresses);
Karen Carpenter (singer), Karen Horney
(psychoanalyst). **Caren, Carin, Caryn, Kari,
Karin.**

Kari (263) Norwegian form of **Karen** or
Katherine.

Karina (238) Latin feminine form of Greek
karinos, "witty," or form of **Carina,** Italian
"dear one." **Carina, Karena.**

Karla (190) Feminine form of **Carl** (and see
Carly). Carla Anderson Hills (U.S. secretary
of housing and urban development), Karla
Jay (author), Carla Tortelli (character on TV
series *Cheers*). **Carla.**

Kate (279) Form of **Catherine** and
Katharine. Kate Millett (feminist
philosopher); Kate Mulgrew, Kate Nelligan
(actresses).

Katherine (10) Ancient Greek *Aikaterina*, unknown meaning. Spelling with *K* was the original form; the Romans substituted Latin *C* for the original Greek *K*. Catherine Deneuve, Katharine Hepburn, (actresses); Katherine Anne Porter (author). **Catherine, Cathryn, Karen, Kat, Kate, Kath, Katharine, Katheryn, Kathleen, Kathrine, Kathryn, Kathy, Katie, Kitty.**

Kathleen (100) Irish Gaelic *Caitlin*, from old French *Cateline*. (See **Katlyn**). Kathleen Turner (actress). **Cathleen**.

Kathy (412) Form of **Katherine**. Kathy Bates (actress). **Cathy, Kathie**.

Katie (50) Form of **Katherine**. Katie Couric (TV newscaster). **Katey, Kati, Katy.**

Katlyn (170) Middle English *Catlyn*, from Old French *Cateline*, which was a form of **Katherine**. In Ireland the same name became **Caitlin** and **Kathleen**. **Catlin, Catlynn, Katlin, Katlynn.**

Katrina (120) Germanic and Scots Gaelic variation of **Catharina**, a Latin form of **Katherine. Catrina**.

Kayla (11) Modern creation based on **Kay;** short form of **Michaela;** or Yiddish form of **Kelila**, Hebrew "crown of laurel." **Calah, Cayla, Kaela, Kaila, Kala, Kaylah.**

Kaylee (66) Usually a modern creation, **Kay + Lee,** though forms **Caley, Kaley,** and **Kayley** can be from *Cailly,* a Norman French place name meaning "forest," or Manx (a Celtic language) *Caoladh,* "slender." **Cailey, Caley, Caylee, Kaeleigh, Kailee, Kaileigh, Kaily, Kalee, Kaleigh, Kaley, Kalie, Kayleigh, Kayley, Kayli, Kaylie.**

Kaylyn (134) **Kay + Lynn,** short form of **Caitlin,** or Irish Gaelic *Caelainn,* "slender lady." **Caylin, Kaelin, Kaelyn, Kailyn, Kalyn, Kalynn, Kaylan, Kaylen, Kaylin, Kaylynn.**

Keely (379) Irish Gaelic *cadhla,* "graceful," or *ceile,* "companion." Keely Garfield (dancer), Keely Smith (singer). **Keeley, Keelie, Keily, Keylee, Kiely.**

Keisha (175) Origin unknown; perhaps from *nkisa,* a Bobangi (Central African language) word meaning "favorite." Keshia Knight-Pulliam (actress). **Kecia, Keesha, Kesha, Keshia, Keysha, Kiesha, Kisha.**

Kelly (33) Derivation same as boy's name **Kelly.** Kelly McGillis (actress). **Kell, Kellee, Kelley, Kelli, Kellie.**

Kelsey (32) Probably Old English *ceol* [ship] + *sige* [victory]. **Kelci, Kelcie, Kelcy, Kellsey, Kelsea, Kelsee, Kelsi, Kelsie.**

Kendall (319) Derivation same as boy's name **Kendall. Kendell, Kendyl.**

Kendra (107) Probably a blend of **Kendrick** and **Sandra. Kendrah.**

Kenya (477) Name of country in central east Africa. **Kenia, Kenyah.**

Keri (162) Variation of masculine **Kerry,** Irish place name. Keri Hulme (author), Kerry Tucker (mystery writer). **Kerri, Kerrie, Kerry.** (See **Kerry** in section on popular boys' names.)

Kia (473) Origin unknown; perhaps a short form of **Kiana** or **Kiara.** Kia Penso (literary critic). **Kea, Keia, Keya.**

Kiana (220) Variation of Qiana, computer-generated trade name for a commercially made silklike fabric. **Keanna, Keiona, Keonna, Keyana, Keyanna, Keyona, Keyonna, Kiona, Kionna.**

Kiara (140) Variation of **Chiara,** a modern Italian name from *chiaro,* "clear." **Chiara, Keara, Keiara, Kieara.**

Kierra (205) African-American creation blending sounds of **Kiana** or **Kiara** with **Sierra** or **Tierra. Keyairra, Kiera.**

Kiersten (278) Swedish form of **Kirsten. Keerstin, Keirsten, Keirstyn, Kierstin.**

Kimberly (39) Old English *Cyneburh-leah,* "Cyneburgh's meadow." Cyneburgh was an

Old-English woman's name meaning "royal fort." Kim Basinger, Kim Stanley (actresses); Kimberly Elliott (economic historian). **Kim, Kimber, Kimberlee, Kimberli, Kimbra, Kimmie.**

Kira (264) Probably an American variation of **Ciara** or **Keira,** feminine forms of **Ciaran** or **Kieran,** which derive from Irish Gaelic *ciar,* "black," Irish saint name. **Keera, Keira, Keyra, Kirra.**

Kirsten (105) Danish and Norwegian form of **Christina.** Kirsten Culver (speed skier), Kirsten Flagstad (opera singer). **Kersten, Kerstin, Kiersten, Kirstie, Kirstyn.**

Kirstie (269) Form of **Christina** or **Kirsten.** Kirstie Alley (actress). **Kirsti, Kirsty.**

Krista (99) German, Czech, and Estonian form of **Christina.** Christa McAuliffe (teacher and astronaut). **Christa, Crista, Krysta.**

Kristen (24) Norwegian form of **Christina** or **Christian.** In Norway **Kristen** is the male form and **Kristin** the female, but in the U.S. both are used for girls, with **Kristen** being slightly more common. Became widely used due to popularity of Norwegian novelist Sigrid Undset's book, *Kristin Lavransdatter,* published in 1922. Kristen Morrow (furniture designer). **Christen, Christin, Cristin, Kristan, Kristen, Kristi, Kristin, Kristyn, Krysten, Krystin.**

Kristy (67) Short form of **Kristen,
Christina,** or **Christine.** Kristy McNichol
(actress), Kristi Yamaguchi (figure skater).
**Christi, Christie, Christy, Cristy, Krista,
Kristi, Kristie, Krysti.**

Kyla (397) Feminine form of **Kyle. Kylah.**

Kylie (103) Feminine form of **Kyle,** or
aboriginal Australian *kylie,* "boomerang."
Kylie Minogue (Australian singer). **Keilly,
Kiley, Kylee, Kyley, Kyly.**

Kyra (431) Feminine form of Greek *kyrios,*
"lord." Kyra Sedgwick (actress).

Lacey (83) Old English *Laci,* from *Lassy,*
"Lascius' estate," French place name. Lacy J.
Dalton (singer). **Laci, Lacie, Lacy, Laycee.**

Lakeisha (228) African-American creation
combining *La-* + **Keisha. Lakeasha, Lakesha,
Lakeshia, Lakisha, Likesha.**

Laken (499) Usually from a medieval short
form of **Lawrence,** but sometimes from
Leyke, a Yiddish form of **Leah.** Laken
Lockridge (character on TV series *Santa
Barbara*). **Laiken, Lakin.**

Lara (435) Probably a short form of **Larissa.**
Lara (major character in book and movie *Dr.
Zhivago*), Lara Flynn Boyle (actress). **Larra.**

Larissa (372) Russian form of Latin *hilaris,*
"laughing, cheerful." Larissa Fontaine
(gymnast). **Larrissa, Laryssa.**

Lashay (486) Modern creation, *La-* + **Shay.**
Lashae, Lashai, Lashaye, Lashea, Leshay.

Lashonda (500) African-American creation,
La- + *-sh-* + *-onda.* **Lashanda.**

Latasha (250) Modern creation, *La-* +
Tasha. Latosha, Letasha, Litasha, L'Tasha.

Latifah (403) Arabic "pleasant, benign,
gentle." Queen Latifah (rap musician).
Lateefa, Lateefah, Lateifa, Lateifah, Latifa.

Latoya (223) African-American creation, *La-*
+ **Toya,** a Mexican form of Victoria; or
perhaps based on the word "toy." LaToya
Jackson (singer). **Latoyia.**

Laura (42) Feminine form of **Lawrence,**
Latin "laurel." Laura Branigan (singer),
Laura San Giacomo (actress), Laura Ingalls
Wilder (author). **Lauren, Laurene, Laurette,**
Laurie, Lora, Loren, Loretta, Lori.

Laurel (434) Old French *lorier,* Latin *laurus,*
"bay-tree." Laurel Thatcher Ulrich
(historian).

Lauren (12) Feminine form of **Lawrence.**
Lauren Bacall (actress). **Lauran, Laurin,**
Lauryn, Lawren.

Leah (72) Origin unclear; perhaps Hebrew
"languid" or "wild cow," or Assyrian "ruler."
Lea Thompson (actress). **Lea, Lia.**

Leanna (258) English form of **Liana,** Italian short form of **Juliana** or **Emiliana;** or from **Lee** + **Anna.** Liana Bolis (biologist). **Leana, Leighanna, Liana, Lianna.**

Leanne (224) **Lea** + **Anne.** Leann Jones (trap shooter). **Leann, Leeanne, Liane.**

Leigh (303) Old English *leah,* "glade, clearing, pasture." Leigh Taylor-Young (actress). **Lee, Lei**.

Lena (341) Usually a form of **Helena,** Latin form of **Helen,** though also a variation of **Adeline, Arlene,** or **Magdalena** (see **Madeline**). Lena Horne (vocalist), Lina Wertmuller (movie director). **Leena, Lina.**

Leslie (109) Derivation same as boy's name **Leslie.** Leslie Caron, Lesley Ann Warren (actresses); Leslie Uggams (singer). **Lesleigh, Lesley, Lesli, Lesly, Lezlie.**

Letitia (199) Latin *laetitia,* "gladness." Letitia Baldridge (writer on etiquette). **Laetitia, Lateisha, Latisha, Leititia, Leticia, Lettice, Lettie.**

Lillian (329) Variation of **Lily.** Lillian Gish (actress), Lillian Hellman (dramatist). **Lilian.**

Lily (398) Greek *leirion,* through Latin *lilium,* and Old English *lilie,* "lily"; also German **Lili,** a form of **Elizabeth.** Lily Tomlin (comedienne), Lili Zanuck (director). **Lil, Lili, Lilli, Lillian, Lillie, Lilly.**

Linda (200) Spanish "beautiful"; German "serpent." Linda Evans (actress), Linda Ronstadt (singer). **Lindy, Lynd, Lynda.**

Lindsey (27) Old English place name "Lincoln's island" from celtic *linn* [lake] + *coln* [Roman colony] + *eg* [island]. Lindsay Crouse, Lindsay Wagner (actresses). **Lindsay, Lindsy, Linsey, Lyndsay, Lyndsey, Lyndsi, Lyndsie, Lyndsy.**

Linsey (309) Form of **Lindsey. Linsay, Linsy, Linzy, Lynnsey, Lynsey, Lynzi.**

Lisa (70) Variation of **Elizabeth.** Lisa Bonet (actress), Lisa Stansfield (singer). **Leesa, Leisa, Lise, Lisetta, Lissette.**

Lissette (419) French form of **Elizabeth** and **Lisa.** Lisette Model (photographer). **Lisette, Lissett, Lizet, Lizette, Lizzette**.

Loren (333) Form of **Laura. Lorin, Lorren, Loryn.**

Lori (306) Form of **Laura;** also from **Lorraine,** French place name, itself derived from **Lothair,** Old German *hlut* [loud] + *heri* [army]. Lori McNeil (tennis player), Lori Singer (actress). **Lorri, Lorrie, Lorry**.

Lucy (387) Latin feminine form of *Lucius,* a Roman given name, probably from *lux,* "light." Lucy Ricardo (title character in TV series *I Love Lucy*). **Luce, Luciana, Lucie, Lucille, Lucinda, Lucita.**

Lydia (191) Greek place name *Lydios* (an ancient part of Asia Minor). Lydia Pulsipher (cultural geographer). **Lidia, Lyda.**

Lynn (463) Old English *hlynn*, "stream" or Celtic *linn*, "pool." Lynn Cooper (psychologist), Lynn Thigpen (actress). **Lin, Linn, Lyn, Lynne.**

Mackenzie (129) Derivation same as boy's name **Mackenzie.** Mackenzie Phillips (actress). **McKenzie, Makensie, Makenzie, Mickenzie.**

Macy (314) English surname from *Macey*, French place name, "Maccius's estate"; now associated with the department store chain. Macy Spectra Forrester (character on TV series *The Bold and the Beautiful*). **Macey, Maci, Macie.**

Madeline (128) French form of **Magdalene,** "woman of Magdala"; Greek place name from Hebrew *migdal*, "high tower." Madeline Kahn (actress), Madeleine L'Engle (author). **Madalyn, Madelaine, Madeleine, Madelin, Madelon, Madelyn, Magda, Magdalena, Magdalene, Maude.**

Madison (159) Middle English *Madyson*, either "son of Matthew" or "son of Maud." **Maddison, Madisan, Madisen.**

Maegan (285) American variation of **Megan,** blending it with sound of **May.** **Magan, Magon, Maigen, Maygen, Maygon.**

Maggie (237) Form of **Margaret** or **Magdalene.** Maggie Smith (actress), Maggie Kuhn (founder, Gray Panthers). **Maggi, Maggy**.

Mallory (125) Old French *maloret,* "the unlucky one." Mallory Keaton (character on TV series *Family Ties*). **Malerie, Mallary, Mallori, Mallorie, Malorie.**

Mandy (286) Form of **Amanda.** "Mandy" (title of popular song recorded by Barry Manilow). **Mandi, Mandie**.

Marah (364) Hebrew "bitter." Mara Wagner (tennis player). **Mara, Mari.**

Marcy (401) Short form of **Marsha;** or from *Marcy,* a Norman-French place name. Marcy Kaptur (member of Congress). **Marcee, Marci, Marcie.**

Margaret (104) Greek *margaritos,* "pearl." Margaret Fuller (critic), Margaret Mead (anthropologist), Margaret Thatcher (prime minister of Great Britain). **Gretchen, Madge, Mag, Maggie, Marga, Margarethe, Margarita, Marge, Margie, Margot, Margret, Marguerite, Marjorie, Meg, Megan, Peg, Peggy, Rita.**

Maria (76) Latin form of **Mary.** Maria Conchita Alonso (actress), Maria Montessori (educator), Maria Muldaur (singer), Maria Von Trapp (heroine in *The Sound of Music*). **Marea, Mariah, Mia, Mitzi.**

Mariah (219) English variation of **Maria.**
Best known from song "They Call the Wind
Mariah." Mariah Carey (singer).

Marie (218) French form of **Mary.** Marie
Curie (chemist).

Marilyn (436) Variation of **Mary Ellen;** also
Mary + Lynn. Marilyn Monroe (actress),
Marilyn Pearsall (philosopher).

Marina (384) Possibly feminine form of
Latin *marinus* "of the sea." Marina Sirtis
(actress), Marina Whitman (economist).
Mareena, Marena.

Marisa (251) Spanish and German blend of
Maria with **Elisa** or **Luisa.** Marisa Tomei
(actress). **Maresa.**

Marisela (495) Spanish blend of **Maria** and
Isabela. Maricela, Marisella, Marizela.

Marissa (94) Modern blend of **Marisa** and
Melissa. Marissa Chibas (actress). **Maryssa,
Merissa.**

Marsha (493) Feminine form of *Marcius,*
Latin family name derived from Mars, the
god of war. Marsha Norman (dramatist),
Marsha Warfield (comedienne). **Marcia,
Marcy.**

Martha (289) Aramaic feminine form of
mar, "a lord." Martha Graham (dancer),

Martha Washington (spouse of President
Washington). **Marta, Marthe, Marthine,
Marty, Mattie, Patty.**

Mary (43) English form of Hebrew **Miriam**,
unknown meaning, though "child we wished
for" and "seeress" are possibilities. Mary
Lunn (mechanical engineer); Mary Tyler
Moore, Mary Steenburgen, (actresses). **Mair,
Maire, Mari, Maria, Mariam, Marian, Marie,
Marika, Marilyn, Mariquita, Marita, Marya,
Maura, Maureen, Miriam, Moll, Molly, Poll,
Polly.**

Maryann (430) **Mary** + **Ann.** Marianne
Faithfull (singer). **Marianne, Maryanne.**

Maura (415) Irish Gaelic *Maire*, form of
Mary. Maura O'Connell (singer), Maura
Sheehan (artist).

Maureen (426) Irish Gaelic *Mairin*, form of
Mary. Maureen McCormick, Maureen
O'Hara, (actresses); Maureen McGovern
(singer). **Maurene, Maurine, Moreen.**

Maya (305) Probably modern form of **Maia,**
from Greek "wet-nurse" or Latin "great,
major"; in Greek and Roman mythology the
name of the mother of Hermes or Mercury.
Maya Angelou (author and actress), Maya
Ying Lin (designer of the Vietnam Memorial
in Washington, D.C.). **Maia, Mya.**

Megan (6) Welsh form of **Margaret.**
Spellings such as **Maegen, Meagan,** and
Meghan result from American efforts to
make the name seem Irish, but it is not an
Irish name. Megan Follows (actress),
Meghann Cleary (character in novel *The
Thornbirds*). **Maegan, Meagan, Meagen,
Meaghan, Meggan, Meghan, Meghann,
Megin.**

Melanie (96) French form of *melaina*, Greek
"dark, black." Melanie Griffith (actress),
Melanie Wilkes (character in novel *Gone With
the Wind*). **Melani, Melany, Mellanie, Mellie,
Melonie, Melony.**

Melinda (161) Creation of eighteenth-
century English poets, probably by blending
Melissa and **Belinda.** Melinda Dillon
(actress). **Linda, Lindy, Malinda, Melynda,
Mindy.**

Melisa (469) Spanish form of **Melissa.
Malesa, Malisa, Mellisa.**

Melissa (29) Greek *melissa*, "honey" or
"honey bee." Melissa Etheridge (singer),
Melissa Gilbert (actress). **Lissa, Malissa,
Melisa, Melitta, Mellissa, Melyssa, Missy.**

Melody (275) Greek *meloidia*, "choral
singing." Melody Anderson (actress).
Melodie.

Mercedes (151) Spanish "mercies" from
Maria de Mercedes, "Mary of Mercies."

Mercedes Jellinek (inspiration for name of German automobile company); Mercedes Ruehle, Mercedes McCambridge (actresses). **Mercedez, Mersadies.**

Meredith (194) Welsh *Maredudd*, "great lord." A male name in Wales, but female in England and America. Meredith Baxter (actress), Meredith Vieira (TV journalist). **Meredee, Meredyth, Merideth, Meridith, Merrie.**

Mia (283) Italian "my, mine," or Swedish form of **Maria.** Mia Dillon, Mia Farrow (actresses). **Mea.**

Micah (427) Derivation same as boy's name **Micah.** Mica Paris (singer). **Mica, Mika, Mikah, Myca, Mycah, Myka, Mykah.**

Michaela (116) Feminine form of **Michael,** Hebrew "Who is like the Lord?" Michaela Fukacova (cellist). **Makayla, McKayla, Micaela, Michelle, Miguela, Mikaela, Mikala, Mikayla, Mikki.**

Michal (487) Hebrew "brook," or a feminine form of **Michael.** Michael Learned (actress), Michal Shahaf (gymnast). **Michael, Mikal, Mychal.**

Michelle (28) French feminine form of **Michael.** "Michelle" (title of song recorded by the Beatles); Michelle Pfeiffer, Michele Lee (actresses). **Mechelle, Michel, Michele, Michell.**

Mindy (337) Form of **Melinda**. Mindy Carson (singer). **Mindee, Mindi.**

Miranda (85) Latin "admirable." Miranda Richardson (actress). **Maranda, Meranda, Mira, Myranda, Randa, Randi.**

Miriam (370) Original Hebrew form of **Mary**. Miriam Wallace Ferguson (governor of Texas), Miriam Makeba (singer). **Mimi, Myriam.**

Misha (433) Russian short form of male name **Michael**, used in the U.S. for girls. **Meesha, Meisha, Mischa.**

Misty (209) Old English *mistig*, "lightly foggy," with modern American informal meaning of "sentimental." Misty Rowe (actress). **Misti, Mistie, Mysti.**

Molly (74) Form of **Mary**. Molly Ivins (columnist), Molly Ringwald (actress). **Mollee, Mollie.**

Monica (93) Origin unknown, may be derived from Greek *monos*, "alone," or Latin "advise," or may be of North African origin. Monica Seles (tennis player). **Monika, Monique.**

Monique (160) French form of **Monica**. Monique Wittig (author). **Moneek, Monike.**

Morgan (57) Welsh, either *mor* [sea] or *mawr* [great] + *can* [bright]. Morgan Fairchild (actress). **Morgana, Morgen, Morgin.**

Nadia (443) Ukrainian form of Russian *nadezhda*, "hope." Nadia Boulanger (composer and conductor), Nadia Comaneci (Olympic gymnast). **Nadine, Nadja, Nadya.**

Nakia (491) Origin unknown, may be a short form of **Nikita.** Nakia (male title character in TV series). **Nackia, Nakiyyah, Nekia, Nikia, Nikkia.**

Nakisha (494) African-American creation, **Nakia** + *-isha*. **Nakeisha, Nakesha, Nakishia, Nikisha, Nikkesha.**

Nancy (217) Medieval English form of **Ann** or **Agnes.** Nancy Kassebaum (U.S. senator), Nancy Lopez (golfer). **Nan, Nance, Nanci, Nancie, Nannie.**

Naomi (297) Hebrew "pleasantness." Naomi Judd (singer), Naomi Wolfe (author). **Naoma, Noemi, Noemie.**

Natalia (396) Russian and Latin form of **Natalie.** Natalia Gutman (cellist). **Natalya, Natasha, Talia**.

Natalie (62) French form of Latin *natale*, "birthday"; originally given to girls born on Christmas day. Natalie Barney (novelist), Natalie Cole (singer). **Nat, Natalee, Natali, Natalia, Nataline, Nataly, Nathalie.**

Natasha (87) Russian variation of **Natalia.** Natasha (character on TV cartoon series *Rocky and His Friends*). **Natosha, Netasha, Tasha.**

Nicole (17) French feminine form of
Nicholas. Nicole Hollander (cartoonist),
Nicole Kidman (actress). **Nichol, Nichole,
Nicol, Nicolette, Nicolle, Nikita, Nikki,
Nikole.**

Nicolette (405) Form of **Nicole.** Nicollette
Sheridan (actress). **Nicollette.**

Nikita (362) Russian form of Greek
Aniketos, "unconquerable," used in the U.S.
as a form of **Nicole.** *La Femme Nikita* (title
of French film). **Nakia, Nakita, Nekita,
Nikeeta, Nikketa, Nikkita.**

Nikki (195) Form of **Nicole.** Nikki Giovanni
(poet). **Nicki, Nicky, Niki, Nikkie**.

Nina (239) Russian and Italian form of **Ann**
or **Antonina.** Nina Simone (singer), Nina
Totenberg (radio journalist). **Neena, Nena,
Ninette**.

Noelle (414) French feminine form of **Noel.**

Olivia (82) Italian form of Latin *oliva,* "olive
tree." Olivia de Havilland (actress), Olivia
Newton-John (singer and actress). **Livia,
Livvie, Oliva, Olive, Olivette, Ollie.**

Paige (78) Old French "knight's servant."
Paige O'Hara (singer, voice of Belle in film
Beauty and the Beast). **Page.**

Pamela (243) Created by sixteenth-century
English poet Philip Sidney, possibly from

Greek *pan-melos,* "all honey." Pamela (title character of Samuel Richardson novel), Pamela Tiffin (actress). **Pam, Pamella, Pammie.**

Paris (483) Capital city of France, from *Parisii,* name of a tribe in ancient Gaul (modern France and some adjacent areas). Parris Afton Bonds (romance novelist). **Parris.**

Patrice (422) French form of **Patricia.** Patrice Munsel (singer). **Patreece, Patrise.**

Patricia (106) Feminine form of **Patrick,** Latin "member of the nobility." Patricia Neal (actress), Patricia Schroeder (member of Congress). **Pat, Patrice, Patrisha, Patrizia, Patsy, Patty, Trisha.**

Paula (334) Feminine form of **Paul,** Latin "small." Paula Abdul (singer), Paula Gunn Allen (Native American author). **Paola, Paulette, Paulina, Pauline.**

Porsha (226) Form of *Porcia,* feminine of *Porcis,* Roman clan name of unknown meaning. Today often associated with Porsche, the German sports car. Portia P. James (historian). **Porche, Porchia, Porscha, Porsche, Porshia, Portia.**

Precious (368) Middle English *preciose,* from Latin *pretiosus,* "valuable, costly." Precious Wilson (British singer and dancer). **Preshus.**

Priscilla (247) Latin *Priscus,* "ancient," a
Roman family name. Priscilla Dalmas
(architect), Priscilla Presley (actress).
Pricilla, Pris, Priscila, Prissie.

Quanisha (439) African-American creation,
Qua- + *-n-* + *-isha.* **Kwaneisha, Quaneesha,
Quanesha, Quaneshia, Quinesha, Quinnesha.**

Rachel (16) Hebrew "ewe." Rachel Carson
(biologist), Rachel Ward (actress). **Rachael,
Rachal, Racheal, Rachelle, Rae, Raechel,
Raquel.**

Rachelle (229) Form of **Rachel. Rachele,
Rachell, Shelley.**

Randi (281) Form of **Miranda;** or feminine
form of **Randolf,** Old English "shield-wolf."
Randi Ryterman (economist). **Randee,
Randie, Randy.**

Raquel (244) Spanish form of **Rachel.**
Raquel Welch (actress). **Racquel.**

Raven (183) Old English *hraefn,* "raven."
Raven-Symone (actress). **Raeven, Ravyn.**

Rebecca (21) Hebrew *Ribqah,* uncertain
meaning, perhaps "heifer" or "yoke."
Rebecca DeMornay (actress), Rebecca
Latimer Felton (first woman U.S. senator),
Dame Rebecca West (novelist). **Becca, Becky,
Rabecca, Rebeca, Rebecah, Rebeccah,
Rebekah, Rebekka, Rivka.**

Regina (256) Latin *regina*, "queen." Regina Taylor (actress). **Gina, Regan, Rena, Reyna.**

Renee (154) French form of Latin *renata*, "to be born again, renew." Renee Taylor (actress and writer). **Renae, Renay, Rene, Renea.**

Reyna (429) Spanish form of **Regina. Raina, Rayna, Reina.**

Rhiannon (446) Celtic *Rigantona*, "great queen," name of a goddess in Welsh mythology who gave up immortality to marry a human. **Reannen, Reannon, Rheannan, Rhianon, Riannon.**

Rhonda (423) Form of *Rhondda*, Welsh river name from Celtic "noisy one." Rhonda Fleming (actress). **Ronda.**

Rikki (425) Feminine form of **Ricky.** Rikki Lake (actress). **Ricki, Rickie, Riki.**

Riley (411) Derivation same as boy's name **Riley. Rylee, Rylie.**

Robin (135) Medieval form of **Robert,** used for girls since about 1940. Robin Wright (journalist). **Robyn.**

Rochelle (330) French "little rock." Rochelle Klein (advertising executive). **Rochel, Rochette, Roshelle, Shelley.**

Rosa (371) Latin "rose." Rosa Bonheur (painter), Rosa Parks (civil rights activist).

Rose (284) English form of *rosa,* Latin "rose," or Old German *Hrodohaidis,* "famous." Rose Kennedy (matriarch), Dame Rose Macaulay (novelist). **Rosa, Rosalie, Roselle, Rosetta, Rosie, Rosina, Rosita.**

Rosemary (490) **Rose + Mary.** Rosemary Casals (tennis player).

Roxanne (391) Persian *Raokhshna,* "dawn." Roxanne (character in Rostand's drama *Cyrano de Bergerac*), Roxanne Kuter Williamson (architectural historian). **Roxane, Roxann, Roxanna, Roxie.**

Ruby (381) Latin *rubinus lapis,* "red stone." Ruby Keeler (actress and dancer). **Rubi, Rubie, Rubye.**

Ruth (320) Hebrew "companion." Ruth Benedict (anthropologist). **Rue, Ruthie.**

Ryan (489) Derivation same as boy's name **Ryan.**

Sabrina (127) Roman name of legendary goddess of the Severn River in England. Sabrina LeBeauf (actress). **Sabrena, Sebrina, Zabrina.**

Sade (345) Short form of **Folashade,** Yoruba (Nigeria) "honor confers a crown." Sade (British-Nigerian singer who pronounces her name "shar-day"). **Charde, Shadae, Shardae, Shardai, Sharday, Sharde.**

Sadie (316) Form of **Sarah. Sada, Saydie.**

Sally (369) Form of **Sarah.** Sally Field (actress), Sally Ride (astronaut). **Sal, Sallie.**

Samantha (7) A colonial American creation, probably combining **Sam** with -*antha*, the feminine form of Greek *anthos*, "flower." Samantha (character on TV series *Bewitched*), Samantha Mathis (actress). **Manthy, Sam, Samanthy, Sammantha, Sammie.**

Sandra (206) Form of **Alexander,** Greek "defender of men." Sandra Dee (actress), Sandra Day O'Connor (U.S. Supreme Court justice). **Sandy.**

Sandy (476) Form of **Sandra.** Sandy Dennis (actress). **Sandee, Sandi, Sandie.**

Sarah (5) Hebrew "princess." Sarah Caldwell (conductor), Sara Gilbert (actress). **Cera, Sadie, Sally, Sara, Sari, Sarita.**

Sasha (176) Russian form of **Alexandra. Sacha, Sascha.**

Savannah (132) Taino (Caribbean Native American) *zabana*, "meadow"; also name of river and city in Georgia. **Savana, Savanna.**

Selena (308) Greek "the moon." Selena Trieff (artist). **Celena, Celina, Salina, Selene, Selina.**

Serena (363) Feminine form of Latin *serenus*, "calm." **Cerena, Sarena, Sarina, Serina.**

Shaina (139) Yiddish "beautiful." Shana Alexander (columnist). **Shaine, Shana, Shayna.**

Shakira (432) Arabic "thankful, grateful." **Shaakira, Shakeera, Shakeira, Shakirah, Shakirra, Shekirah.**

Shameka (389) African-American creation, *Sha-* + *-mika* from **Tamika. Chameka, Shameika, Shamica, Shamika, Shemeka, Shemika.**

Shanae (294) African-American creation, blend of **Chanel** and **Renee. Chanay, Shanay, Shanaye, Shanee.**

Shanice (299) African-American creation, *Shan-* from **Shannon** or **Chanel** + *-ice.* Shanice Wilson (singer). **Chanise, Shanece, Shaneice, Shanice, Shaniece, Shanise, Shenice, Shenise.**

Shanika (324) African-American creation, *Shan-* + *-ika.* **Chanika, Shaneka, Shanneika, Sheneka, Shenika, Shinika, Shnika.**

Shaniqua (245) African-American creation, *Shan-* + *-iqua.* **Shaneequa, Shanequa, Shaniequa, Shanikwa.**

Shanna (326) Form of **Shannon** or **Shaina.** Shanna Reed (actress). **Shana, Shannah.**

Shannon (64) Name of a river in Ireland, from a Celtic word meaning "the ancient god." Shannon Garst (author), Shannon

Miller (gymnast). **Channon, Shanna, Shannen, Shannyn, Shanon, Shanyn.**

Shante (268) African-American creation, perhaps related to French *enchante,* "enchanted." **Chantay, Chante, Chonte, Shantae, Shantay, Shontae, Shontay.**

Sharon (270) Hebrew "a plain," Biblical place name. Sharon Gless (actress), Sharon Maczko (artist). **Shari, Sharron, Sherri, Sherry.**

Shawna (141) Feminine form of **Sean** or **Shawn. Shauna, Shaunna, Shawnna.**

Shawnee (466) Name of a Native American nation, used as basis for feminine form of **Shawn. Shaunee, Shauni, Shawnie.**

Shayla (231) Form of **Sheila. Shaela, Shaila, Shala, Shaylah.**

Shaylee (421) Modern creation, **Shay** (see **Shea**) + **Lee. Shaelee, Shailey, Shalee, Shalie, Shayleigh, Shayli.**

Shaylyn (452) Modern creation, **Shay** (see **Shea**) + **Lynn. Shaelyn, Shalynn, Shaylin, Shaylynn, Shealynn.**

Shea (344) Derivation same as boy's name **Shea. Shae, Shay, Shaye.**

Sheena (343) Scottish Gaelic *Sine,* form of **Jane.** Sheena Easton (singer). **Sheenagh, Shena, Sine.**

Sheila (346) Irish Gaelic *Sile,* form of
Cecilia. Sheila Graham (writer), Sheila Young
(speed skater). **Shayla, Sheelagh, Sheelah,
Sheilah, Shela, Shelia, Shiela.**

Shelby (84) English place name, perhaps
meaning "village on a ledge" or "willow
village." **Shelbey, Shelbi, Shelbie.**

Shelley (288) Old English *Selleg,* "clearing
on a ledge," a place name; or form of
Michelle, Rochelle, and similar base names.
Shelley Long (actress). **Shel, Shelli, Shelly.**

Sherika (470) African-American creation,
Sher- from **Sharon** or **Sherry** + *-ika.* **Charika,
Cherika, Shareeka, Sharika, Shereka.**

Sherry (214) Variation of **Sharon** or **Cherie.**
Sherry Lansing (film executive), Shari Lewis
(ventriloquist). **Cheri, Shari, Sheri, Sherri,
Sherrie.**

Shirley (428) Old English *scirleah,* "bright
clearing" or "shire meadow," a place name.
Shirley MacLaine (actress), Shirley Chisholm
(member of Congress). **Shirlee, Shirlene,
Shirly.**

Sierra (73) Spanish *sierra,* "saw-tooth
mountain range." **Ciera, Cierra, Seairra,
Siera.**

Simone (246) French feminine form of
Simon, Hebrew "he heard"; or Greek "snub
nosed." Simone de Beauvoir (writer), Simone
Signoret (actress). **Samone, Symone.**

Skye (457) Name of island off west coast of Scotland, first used as a girl's name in 1957 by American novelist Phyllis Whitney for heroine of her book *Skye Cameron.* **Sky.**

Skylar (293) Feminine form of **Skyler. Schuyler, Skyler.**

Sonya (248) Russian form of **Sophia.** Sonja Henie (figure skater), Sonia Johnson (feminist activist). **Sonia, Sonja.**

Sophia (240) Greek "wisdom." Sophia Loren (actress). **Sofia, Sonia, Sophie, Zofia, Zosia.**

Stacey (80) Short form of **Anastasia** or **Eustacia. Stacey, Staci, Stacie, Stasie.**

Stefanie (8) French feminine form of **Stephen,** Greek "crown." Steffi Graf (tennis player), Stefanie Powers (actress). **Estefania, Stefani, Stefanie, Stefany, Steffi, Stephani, Stephany, Stevie.**

Stevie (448) English form of **Stephanie.** Stevie Nicks (singer), Stevie Smith (poet). **Stevi.**

Summer (230) Old English *sumar,* "summer." Summer Sanders (Olympic swimmer). **Sommer.**

Susan (179) Hebrew *shushannah,* "lily." Susan B. Anthony (women's rights advocate); Susan Saint James, Susan Sarandon (actresses). **Sue, Sukie, Susana, Susie, Suzanne, Suzette, Zuzanna.**

Susana (350) Latin form of **Susan**. Susanna Foster (soprano). **Susanna, Susannah, Suzana, Suzanna, Suzannah.**

Suzanne (292) French form of **Susan**. Suzanne Somers (actress).

Sydney (112) Feminine form of **Sidney**, Old English *sidenieg*, "wide, well-watered land," an English place name. **Cydney, Sidney, Sidni, Sydni, Sydnie.**

Sylvia (336) Latin *silva*, "wood." Sylvia Plath (poet). **Silvia, Sylvie.**

Tabitha (110) Aramaic "gazelle." Tabitha King (novelist). **Tabatha, Tabbatha, Tabby, Tabetha, Tabytha.**

Talisha (478) African-American creation, *Ta-* + **Alicia** or **Talia** + *-isha*. **Taleesha, Taleisha, Talicia, Telisha, Tilicia.**

Tamara (169) Hebrew *Tamar*, "palm tree." Tamara Asseyev (movie producer), Tamara Karsavina (dancer). **Tamar, Tamera, Tammara, Tammy, Tamra.**

Tamesha (420) African-American creation, *Tam-* from **Tamika** or **Tamara** + *-isha*. **Tameesha, Tameisha, Tamicia, Tamisha, Temisha, Tomesha, Tomisha.**

Tamika (273) African-American form of Japanese **Tamiko**: *tami* [people] + *-ko* [feminine suffix]. Probably introduced to the U.S. by the 1963 movie *A Girl Named Tamiko*. **Tameika, Tameka, Tamica, Tomeka, Tomika.**

Tammy (355) Form of **Tamara;** or **Tamsin,** British feminine form of **Thomas.** Tammy Wynette (singer). **Tami, Tamie, Tammie.**

Tanisha (177) Origin unknown; perhaps African-American variation of *Tani,* a Hausa (northern Nigeria) name meaning "born on Monday." Ta-Tanisha (actress on TV series *Room 222*). **Taneisha, Tanesha, Taneshea, Taniesha, Tanishia, Tenecia, Teneisha, Tenesha, Tenisha, Tinisha.**

Tanya (262) Russian form of **Tatiana.** Tanya Roberts (actress), Tanya Tucker (singer). **Tania, Tanja, Tonya.**

Tara (69) Gaelic "a crag, high prominent rock"; or form of Latin *terra,* "earth." Tara O'Connor (flutist). **Tarah, Tarra, Tarrah, Tera, Terra.**

Taryn (257) Invented in 1953 by actors Tyrone Power and Linda Christian for their daughter, probably by blending **Tyrone** with the sound of **Karen** or **Sharon,** popular names at the time. **Taren, Tarin, Terran, Teryn.**

Tasha (172) Form of **Natasha. Tashia, Tosha.**

Tatiana (291) Feminine form of *Tatius*, name of a king of the Sabines in ancient Italy, unknown meaning, but popular in Greece and Russia. Tatiana Troyanos (opera singer). **Tanya, Tatianna, Tatyana.**

Tawny (456) Middle English *tauny*, "yellowish brown," first used as a girl's name in 1936 by novelist Donald Henderson Clarke. Tawney Godin Schneider (entertainment reporter). **Tahnee, Tauni, Taunie, Tawnee, Tawney, Tawni, Tawnie.**

Taylor (52) Derivation same as boy's name **Taylor.** Taylor Caldwell (novelist). **Taelor, Tailer, Tayler.**

Terri (298) Usually a form of **Theresa** (and see **Terry** in section on popular boys' names). Teri Garr, Terry Moore (actresses). **Tera, Teri, Terra, Terrie, Terry.**

Tessa (276) Usually a form of **Theresa;** perhaps also a form of *Contessa*, Italian "countess." **Tess, Tessi, Tessie, Tessy.**

Theresa (117) Origin unknown; possibly "woman from Therasia," ancient name for two small Mediterranean islands. Theresa Russell (actress). **Teresa, Terri, Tess, Tessa, Tessie, Therese, Theresia, Thresa, Tracy, Treasa, Tressa, Tressie.**

Tia (235) Spanish *tia,* "aunt," or short form of **Tiara** or **Tiana. Teah, Teia.**

Tiana (241) Cherokee (Native American) form of **Diana,** or German form of **Christiana.** Tiana Bighorse (Native American author), Tiana Lemnitz (opera singer). **Teanna, Teonna, Teyonna, Tia, Tianna.**

Tiara (197) Greek "turban," through Latin "headdress, jeweled coronet." **Tearra, Tia, Tiarra, Tierra.**

Tierra (234) Spanish "earth" or "land"; or form of **Tiara. Teaira, Tiera.**

Tiffany (23) Greek *Theophania,* "revelation of God," name sometimes given to children born on Epiphany (January 6). Tiffany Chin (figure skater), Tiffany (well-known jewelry store). **Teofania, Tifani, Tiffani, Tiffanie, Tiffeny, Tiffiny, Tiffy, Tiphanie, Tyffany.**

Tina (236) Form of names ending in -tina, such as **Christina, Ernestina,** and **Valentina.** Tina Turner (singer). **Teena, Teenie, Tena, Tiny.**

Toni (225) Form of **Antonia.** Toni Morrison (author). **Tonie, Tony.**

Tonya (274) Short form of **Antonia** or form of **Tanya. Tonia.**

Tori (253) Short form of **Victoria.** Tori Amos (singer and songwriter), Tori Thomas (landscape architect). **Torie, Torrey, Torri, Tory.**

Tracy (146) Variation of **Theresa.** Tracy Austin (tennis player), Tracy Chapman (singer). **Tracee, Tracey, Traci, Tracie.**

Trisha (201) Form of **Patricia.** Trisha Yearwood (singer). **Tricia, Trish.**

Tyler (482) Derivation same as boy's name **Tyler.**

Valerie (147) French form of Latin *valere,* "strong." Valerie Bertinelli, Valerie Harper, Valerie Perrine (actresses). **Valarie, Valery.**

Vanessa (77) Created by Jonathan Swift in 1713 poem *Cadenus and Vanessa* to honor his friend Esther VanHomrigh. Vanessa Redgrave (actress). **Vanesa, Venessa.**

Veronica (136) Variation of **Bernice:** Greek *Berenike,* "bringer of victory"; probably modified in ancient times to resemble Latin *vera icon,* "true image." Veronica Hamel (actress). **Veronika.**

Victoria (47) Feminine form of **Victor,** Latin "conqueror." Victoria Jackson (comedienne), Victoria Principal (actress). **Tori, Vic, Vicki, Viktoria.**

Virginia (215) Feminine form of *Virginius,* Latin "virginlike." Virginia Madsen (actress), Virginia Wade (tennis player), Virginia Woolf (novelist). **Ginger, Ginnie, Virginie.**

Wendy (265) Created by J. M. Barrie for his
play *Peter Pan* from baby-talk word "friendy-
wendy." Wendy Hiller (actress), Wendy
Turnbull (tennis player). **Wendee, Wendi,
Wendie.**

Whitley (385) Middle English *Witelay*,
"white glade," from Old English *hwit* [white]
+ *leah* [woods, clearing]. Whitley Gilbert
(character on TV series *A Different World*).
Whitlee, Whitleigh, Whitlie.

Whitney (53) Old English *Wittenheia*, "white
island," from *hwit* [white] + *ey* [island].
Whitney Blake (actress), Whitney Houston
(singer). **Whitnee, Whitni, Whitnie,
Whittany, Whittney.**

Yasmin (386) Arabic form of **Jasmine.**
Yasmin Ramirez (art critic). **Yasemin,
Yasmine, Yasmyn, Yazmin.**

Yesenia (198) Origin unknown, but popular
with Hispanics because of soap-opera
character. **Jesenia, Jessenia, Llesenia,
Yecenia, Yessenia, Yexenia.**

Yolanda (409) Medieval French form of
Iolanthe: Greek *ion* [violet] + *anthos* [flower].
Yolanda King (actress and daughter of
Martin Luther King, Jr.). **Iolande, Jolan,
Jolanda, Jolanta, Yalonda, Yolande, Yolonda.**

Yvette (460) Form of **Yvonne.** Yvette
Mimieux (actress). **Evette, Ivette.**

Yvonne (465) Feminine form of **Yvon,** a variation of **Yves:** Gaulish *iv*, "yew tree." Evonne Goolagong (tennis player), Yvonne De Carlo (actress). **Evonne, Eyvonne, Ivonne, Vonnie, Yvette.**

Zoe (498) Greek "life," originally the Greek translation of **Eve.** Zoe Akins (playwright), Zoe Caldwell (actress). **Zoey.**

Unusual Girls' Names

Ada Form of **Adelaide** or **Adela** or Hebrew *adah,* "ornament." Ada Deer (Native American civil rights activist). **Adah.**

Adora Posssibly Greek "a gift." **Adoree, Dora, Dori, Dorie, Dory.**

Akosua Ewe (Ghana) "born on Sunday." Akosua Busia (actress).

Alberta Feminine form of **Albert,** Old German *athal* [noble] + *bertha* [bright]. Alberta Hunter (singer). **Albertina, Berta, Bertie, Birdie, Elberta.**

Allegra Italian "lively, cheerful, gay, sprightly." Allegra Kent (ballerina).

Antonia Feminine form of **Anthony.** Antonia Novello (U.S. surgeon general). **Andona, Antonina, Toni, Tonia.**

Anuli Ibo (Nigeria) "joy."

Araceli Spanish form of Latin *ara coeli,* "altar of heaven." **Aracelie, Aracelis, Aracely, Araseli, Arasely, Areli.**

Aspen Old English *aespen,* "aspen, poplar." Today associated with ski resort in Colorado.

Audra Usually a form of **Audrey,** but also a Lithuanian name meaning "thunderstorm."

Aziza Swahili (East Africa) "precious."

Belle Latin *bella*, "beautiful" or form of **Isabel**. Belle (heroine of film *Beauty and the Beast*). **Belinda, Bell, Bella.**

Bernadette Feminine form of **Bernard,** Old German "bear" and "brave." Bernadette Peters (singer and actress). **Bernadine, Bernardette, Bernita.**

Birunji Luganda (Uganda) "pretty, perfect thing."

Blossom Old English *blosma*, "flower of a plant." Blossom Rock (actress).

Blythe Old English "blithe, gentle." Blythe Danner (actress). **Blithe.**

Bronwen Welsh *bron* [breast] + *gwen* [white, holy]. **Bronwyn.**

Calista Greek *kallistos*, "most beautiful." **Callista.**

Cleo Greek *kleios*, "praise, fame"; also a form of **Cleopatra.** Cleo Laine (singer). **Clea.**

Cloris Greek *chloris*, "pale green." Cloris Leachman (actress). **Chloris.**

Colette French short form of **Nicolette.** Colette (novelist). **Collette.**

Consuela Spanish from Latin "consolation."
Consuelo Northrup Bailey (Republican Party
official). **Connie, Consolacion, Consuelo.**

Cora Probably Greek *kore*, "girl." First
known usage in James Fenimore Cooper's
novel *The Last of the Mohicans.* Coretta Scott
King (civil rights activist and spouse of
Martin Luther King, Jr.). **Coretta, Cori,
Corina, Corinne.**

Cornelia Latin feminine of *Cornelius*, a
Roman family name, probably from *cornu*, "a
horn." Cornelia Otis Skinner (actress).
Cornela, Cornelle, Nelleke.

Danuta Polish, perhaps a form of Latin
Donata, "given [by God]."

Daphne Greek *daphne*, "laurel tree." Daphne
du Maurier (novelist). **Dafney, Daphney.**

Dayo Yoruba (Nigeria) "joy arrives."

Devnet Irish Gaelic *damhnait*, "fawn."

Dionne Feminine form of **Dion.** Dionne
Warwick (singer). **Dion, Dione.**

Disa Old Norse *dis*, "goddess."

Dixie Latin *dixi*, "I have spoken"; or form of
Dixon, "son of Richard." Dixie Lee Ray
(governor of Washington State). **Dix.**

Dolores Latin *dolere*, "pain, sorrow," referring to Maria de Dolores (a Spanish title for the Virgin Mary). **Delores, Deloris.**

Doris Greek "woman from Doris" (central Greece). Doris Day (actress and singer).

Dreama Appalachian-American creation based on "dream." **Drema.**

Eartha Old English *eorthe*, "earth, ground." Eartha Kitt (singer). **Ertha.**

Edith Old English *eadgyth*, from *ead* [rich] + *gyth* [war]. Edith Head (fashion designer). **Edie, Editha, Edythe.**

Edna Hebrew *ednah*, "delight." Edna St. Vincent Millay (poet).

Eleanor Origin uncertain; perhaps from Greek *eleas*, "mercy," or a form of **Helen.** Eleanor Roosevelt (writer, UN delegate, spouse of President Franklin Roosevelt).

Elsa German form of **Elizabeth.** Elsa Klensch (fashion reporter). **Else, Elsie, Ilsa.**

Enid Welsh *enaid*, "soul." Enid Beaupre (advertising executive).

Estelle French form of Latin *stella*, "star." Estelle Getty (actress). **Estella, Estrela.**

Eugenia Feminine of **Eugene.** Eugenia Rho (choreographer). **Eugenie, Gena, Gene.**

Eustacia Greek *eustachius*, "plentiful, fruitful." **Stacie, Stacy.**

Fawn Middle French *faon*, "young deer," from Latin *feton*, "offspring." **Fawna.**

Fidanka Bulgarian "sapling."

Fiona Scots-Gaelic *fionn*, "fair." Invented in eighteenth century by Scottish poet James Macpherson. Fiona Rae (artist).

Flannery Irish Gaelic *Flannabhra*, "red eyebrows." Flannery O'Connor (writer).

Flora Latin "flower." Flora Lewis (journalist). **Fiorella, Fleur, Flo, Flor.**

Gemma Italian *gemma*, "gem." Gemma Craven (actress). **Jemma.**

Georgia Feminine form of **George,** Greek "farmer." Georgia O'Keeffe (artist).

Giselle French form of *Gisila*, Old German "pledge, hostage." Giselle Fernandez (TV newscaster). **Gisel, Gisela, Gisele, Gisselle.**

Glenda Feminine form of **Glen,** also Welsh *glen* [clean] + *da* [good]. Glenda Jackson (actress).

Gwendolyn Welsh *Gwendolen*, from *gwen* [white] + *dolen* [link, ring]. Gwendolyn Brooks (poet). **Guendolen, Gwen, Gwenda.**

Halima Arabic and Swahili "gentle."

Hara Maricopa (Native American, Arizona) "blaze."

Haunani Hawaiian, "beautiful hibiscus tree."

Hazel Old English *haesel*, "hazel tree." Hazel Bishop (chemist). **Haze.**

Ifetayo Yoruba (Nigeria) "love brings happiness."

Ileana Romanian form of **Helen.** Ileana Ros-Lehtinen (first Cuban-American elected to U.S. Congress).

Ilka Short form of **Ilonka** and **Ilona,** Hungarian forms of **Helen.** Ilka Chase (actress and columnist).

Indira Hindi *Indra*, "India." Indira Gandhi (prime minister of India).

Ingrid Old Norse from *Inge* [a Norse god] + *frid* [pretty]. Ingrid Bergman (actress).

Ione Greek "violet." Ione Skye (actress). **Iona.**

Irene Greek *eirene*, "peace." Irene Dunne (actress). **Irena, Irina.**

Iris Greek *iris*, "rainbow." Iris Murdoch (author). **Irita.**

Iruka Ibo (Nigeria) "the future is supreme."

Isadora Greek "gift of Isis" from *Isis* [goddess of the Nile] + *dorus* [gift]. Isadora Duncan (dancer). **Isidora.**

Ivy Old English *ifig,* "ivy." Ivy Baker Priest (U.S. treasurer).

Jerusha Hebrew "inheritance." Jerusha (character in Michener's novel *Hawaii*).

Jewel Old French *jouel,* "jewel." Jewelle Gomez (poet). **Jewell, Jewelle.**

Jinda Modern creation, **Jean** + **Linda.**

Jovita Feminine form of Latin *Jove,* "Jupiter."

Kaia Estonian form of **Katherine. Kaya.**

Kamaria Swahili (East Africa) "like the moon."

Kirti Marathi (western India) "fame."

Kizuwanda Zaramo (Tanzania) "last-born child."

Kuniko Japanese *kuni* [countryside] + *-ko* [feminine suffix]. Kuniko Miyanaga (sociologist).

Lark Old English *lawerce,* "songbird." Lark McCarthy (TV reporter).

Leona Feminine form of **Leo** or **Leon.** Leona Tyler (psychologist).

Liadan Irish Gaelic, perhaps "grey lady."
Name of famous medieval Irish poet.
Leahdan, Liadaine.

Lila Form of *Lailaa*, Arabic "night." Lila
Valentine (suffragist). **Lyla, Lylah.**

Liv Old Norse *hlif*, "defense"; also modern
Norwegian word for "life." Liv Ullman
(actress).

Liza Form of **Elizabeth.** Liza Minelli (singer
and actress). **Lizette, Lizzie.**

Lois Possibly Greek "the better." Lois
Nettleton (actress).

Lokelani Hawaiian, "heavenly rose."

Loretta Form of **Laura;** also a feminine form
of *Loreto*, "laurels," Italian place name.
Loretta Lynn (singer).

Louise French feminine form of **Louis.** Louise
Fletcher (actress). **Lou, Louisa, Luisa, Lulu.**

Lucille French form of **Lucy.** Lucille Ball
(actress and comedienne).

Lyra Latin "lyre," name of a northern
constellation containing the star Vega.

Maeve Irish Gaelic *mebd*, "intoxicating,"
name of a goddess and a famous warrior
queen in ancient Ireland. Maeve Binchy
(author).

Mairead Irish Gaelic form of **Margaret.**
Mairead Corrigan (1976 Nobel Prize winner
for peace).

Malia Hawaiian language form of **Mary;**
very popular in Hawaii in the 1980s.

Maren Danish form of **Marina.** Maren
Jensen (actress).

Margot French form of **Margaret.** Dame
Margot Fonteyn (ballet dancer). **Margo.**

Marlene German blend of **Maria** and
Magdalene. Marlene Dietrich (actress).
Marlaina, Marlena.

Martina Feminine form of **Martin.** Martina
Navratilova (tennis player).

Merle Latin *merula*, "blackbird." Merle
Oberon (actress). **Myrle.**

Merry Old English *myrige*, "pleasant,
merry." Merry Anders (actress). **Merri,
Merrie.**

Mildred Old English *mild* [gentle] + *thryth*
[strength]. Mildred Dunnock (actress). **Mil,
Millie.**

Miren Basque form of **Mary.**

Mohini Marathi (western India) "the
attractive one."

Mona English form of *Muadnat*, Irish Gaelic "noble one"; also form of **Monica.** Mona Maris (actress). **Monna.**

Muriel Irish Gaelic *Muirgel*, "sea-bright." Muriel Spark (novelist). **Murial, Murielle.**

Nadine French form of **Nadia.** Nadine Gordimer (1991 Nobel Prize winner for literature). **Nadene.**

Nalini Sanskrit (India) "lily." Nalini Nadkarni (biologist).

Neema Swahili (East Africa) "born into prosperous times."

Nerys Feminine form of Welsh *ner*, "lord." Nerys Patterson (archæologist).

Ngozi Ibo (Nigeria) "blessing."

Nichelle Modern blend of **Nicole** and **Michelle.** Nichelle Nichols (actress).

Nora Form of **Honora** or **Eleanor.** Nora Ephron (author). **Norita.**

Noreen Irish form of **Honora,** Latin "honor." Noreen Corcoran (actress).

Norma Latin *norma*, "model" or "pattern." Norma Quarles (newscaster). **Norm.**

Octavia Latin "eighth." Octavia E. Butler (novelist). **Octavie, Ottavia, Tavi.**

Olympia Greek "heavenly," from Mount
Olympus. Olympia Dukakis (actress).
Olimpia, Olympe.

Oprah Form of **Orpah,** an Old Testament
name of unknown meaning. Oprah Winfrey
(actress and TV personality).

Orla Irish Gaelic *Orfhlaith*, "golden princess."

Patience Latin *patientia*, "patience."
Patience Worth (novelist).

Pearl Latin *perna*, "sea mussel," through
Middle English *perle*, "pearl" (gem). Pearl
Bailey (singer).

Penelope Greek, probably "weaver."
Penelope (wife of Odysseus in Homer's
Odyssey). **Penny.**

Phoebe Greek *phoibe*, "the bright one."
Phoebe Cates (actress).

Quintina Feminine form of **Quintin,** Latin
"fifth." **Quenna, Quentilla, Quinna, Quintana.**

Radclyffe Middle English *Radeclyf*, "red
cliff." Radclyffe Hall (British novelist).

Ramona Feminine form of **Ramon,** Spanish
form of **Raymond.** Ramona Banuelos (U.S.
treasurer).

Rehema Swahili (East Africa) "compassion."
Rehema Stephens (basketball player).

Rita Form of **Margarita.** Rita Moreno
(actress). **Reta.**

Rosalind Old German *Roslindis,* probably
from *hroth* [fame] + *lindi* [serpent]. Rosalind
Cartwright (psychologist), Rosalind Russell
(actress).

Rosanne Combination of **Rose** + **Anne.**
Roseanne Arnold (comedienne and title
character in TV series). **Roseann, Roseanne.**

Rowena Uncertain origin, possibly Old
English "famous friend" or Welsh "lance"
and "fair." Rowena Morrill (artist and
illustrator). **Rowe.**

Ruta Lithuanian "rue," a flowering herb.
Ruta Lee (actress).

Salome Hebrew *shalom,* "peace." Salome
Jens (actress). **Salima, Salomee, Salomi.**

Sanura Swahili (East Africa) "kitten."

Sawa Miwok (Native American, California)
"rock."

Scarlett Middle English "deep red." Scarlett
O'Hara (main character in novel *Gone With
the Wind*). **Scarlet.**

Shenandoah Algonquian (Native American)
"spruce stream," name of river and valley in
Virginia known for its beauty.

Siroun Armenian "lovely." **Siran.**

Sive (rhymes with *five*) Irish Gaelic *sabd,* "sweet," a daughter of Maeve, famous warrior queen of Connacht, and an extremely common name in medieval Ireland.

Stella Latin "star." Stella Stevens (actress). **Estelle.**

Sybil Greek *sibulla,* "a woman prophet." Dame Sybil Thorndike (actress). **Sibil.**

Tanith Name of great sky goddess of ancient Carthage. Tanith Lee (science fiction writer).

Tatum Old English *Tatham,* "Tata's homestead." Tatum O'Neal (actress).

Tempest Latin *tempestas,* "weather, storm," through Middle English *tempeste.* First used as a girl's name by Mary Jane Holmes in her 1854 novel *Tempest and Sunshine.* Tempestt Bledsoe (actress). **Tempestt.**

Tesla Croatian surname meaning "adze" or "carpenter." Tesla (rock music band). **Tessla.**

Thea Greek "goddess"; feminine form of **Theo.** Thea Musgrave (composer).

Thema Akan (Ghana) "queen."

Tierney Irish Gaelic *tighearna,* "lord."

Treasure Latin *thesaurus,* "storehouse," through Middle English *tresor,* "wealth."

Tuuli Estonian "wind, breeze."

Una Irish name of unknown meaning; also Latin "one." Una O'Connor (actress). **Oona.**

Ursula Latin *ursa*, "bear." Ursula Andress (actress). **Ursel.**

Vesta Latin "goddess of the hearth." Vesta (blues singer).

Violet Latin *viola*, "violet." Violet Weingarten (screenwriter). **Violeta, Violette.**

Vivian Latin *vivus*, "alive." Vivien Leigh (actress). **Viv, Vivien, Vivienne.**

Wanda Slavic name of uncertain meaning, perhaps "woman of the Vandals." Wanda Hendrix (actress). **Vanda, Vonda.**

Willa Feminine form of **Will** or **William.** Willa Cather (author).

Yoko Japanese *yo-* [positive] + *-ko* [feminine suffix]. Yoko Ono (artist and musician).

Zelia Origin unclear; perhaps Latin "solemn" or Greek "zeal." Zelia Nuttall (archaeologist).

Ziazan Armenian *dziazan*, "rainbow."